INTERNATIONAL DEVELOPMENT IN FOCUS

China's High-Speed Rail Development

Martha Lawrence, Richard Bullock, and Ziming Liu

WORLD BANK GROUP

Contents

Maps

Photos

Tables

Foreword

2018 marked the 40th anniversary of China's "reform and opening up"—a period of high growth and poverty reduction. China's remarkable development was made possible by a wide range of reforms that transformed the economy into a more market-based open economy and through a large-scale infrastructure development program.

China's leadership in transport development started with years of investment in skills and know-how, focused on quality, safety, timely completion, investment benefit, environmental protection, and technical innovation. China has made fantastic progress in developing its transport infrastructure. From 1990 to today, China has added over 120,000 kilometers (km) of railways, 130,000 km of expressways, 3.7 million km of road, and 740,000 km of coastal quay lines to its national transport system.

The World Bank has been China's partner in this journey. In the past three decades, the World Bank has approved more than 110 transportation projects in China, with a total investment of $19 billion. The World Bank has also been a knowledge partner, producing over 15 targeted studies captured in the China Transport Topics series. The World Bank and China's Ministry of Transport have jointly developed the Transport Transformation and Innovation Knowledge Platform (TransFORM) program—a flagship knowledge platform to share Chinese and international transport experiences and facilitate learning within China and other World Bank client countries.

What can other countries learn from China's success? Chinese best practices are very relevant for World Bank clients looking for sustainable solutions to transport development challenges. Through TransFORM, the World Bank is analyzing China's experience in five areas of transport—high-speed rail, highways, urban transport, ports, and inland waterways—to identify lessons that are transferrable from China to other developing countries. This report on high-speed rail is the first in this series.

The report covers a broad range of why, what, and how questions. Since 2008, China has put into operation a high-speed rail network that is larger than all the high-speed networks in the rest of the world put together. This rapid growth makes China worth studying from the "how" perspective: What planning processes, capacity development, business structures, and construction modalities enabled this rapid growth? China's traffic has grown to 1.7 billion passenger trips per year. In an era when many railways face declining patronage, what price and service characteristics make high-speed rail attractive to this large number of passengers? China was the first middle-income country to develop a high-speed railway network and to price the service so that people of all income levels use high-speed rail. Why can China price high-speed rail services affordably and still maintain financial and economic viability?

I encourage you to read the full report to find the answers to these and many other questions.

Binyam Reja, PhD
Practice Manager, Transport Global Practice
Central Asia, China, and Mongolia
The World Bank

Acknowledgments

This report was written by Martha Lawrence, Richard Bullock, and Ziming Liu. It is based on a report prepared by the China Railway Design and Research Institute and reports prepared by the World Bank while providing financing for six Chinese high-speed rail projects. Contributors include Bernard Aritua, Gerald Ollivier, Jit Sondhi, Can Hua Tan, Peishen Wang, Jianping Zhang, and Nanyan Zhou. The team is grateful to Binyam Reja, Transport Global Practice Manager for Central Asia, China, and Mongolia, for his guidance and support in preparing this report.

The team would like to thank the following people for reviewing and commenting on the report: Atul Agarwal, Paul Amos, Federico Antoniazzi, Victor Aragonas, Achal Khare, Lei Nie, and Wei Winnie Wang. All errors are the responsibility of the authors. The team would like to acknowledge the cooperation and information provided to the World Bank team by the China Railway Design and Research Institute and the China Railway Corporation, and the many representatives of local and national government who have shared their views on the development of the Chinese high-speed rail system.

Funding for this report was provided by the China–World Bank Group Partnership Facility (CWPF). The objective of the CWPF is to assist developing member countries of the participating World Bank Group organizations in achieving inclusive and sustainable development. The report will be shared via TransFORM, the Transport Transformation and Innovation Knowledge Platform, jointly convened by the government of China and the World Bank to help make comprehensive transport safer, cleaner, and more affordable for development in China, while sharing Chinese experiences with development partners.

About the Authors

Richard Bullock has over 40 years of experience in the railway sector, covering costing and pricing, project analysis, railway restructuring, and regulatory issues. He has worked on over 50 railways worldwide, in every continent except North America, and has worked in China since 1987. Before becoming an independent consultant, Mr. Bullock was a director of Travers Morgan Australia and, in addition to the World Bank, has worked on projects for several other international institutions. He has worked on seven high-speed rail projects in China with the World Bank, as well as five outside China.

Mr. Bullock has an MA in mathematics from Cambridge University and an MA in operational research from Brunel University.

Martha Lawrence is the leader of the Railways Community of Practice at the World Bank and a team leader for the World Bank's technical assistance and lending programs in China and India. She has over 30 years of experience in the railway sector, with extensive knowledge in railway restructuring, railway finance, and transport regulation. Ms. Lawrence led the development of the World Bank's resource on railway reform, *Railway Reform: A Toolkit for Improving Rail Sector Performance*, and the report *Attracting Capital for Rail Development in China*. She has prepared business, restructuring, and financing plans for railways worldwide and advised private sector investors on over US$8 billion in structured lease financing of transit rolling stock and infrastructure.

Ms. Lawrence has a BA in economics from Northwestern University and an MBA in finance and transportation management from Northwestern University.

Ziming Liu joined the World Bank in 2017 as a transport consultant in the Beijing office. She has been involved in the World Bank's technical assistance and lending programs in China and Central Asia in the transport sector since then. She has contributed to multiple World Bank studies, including the upcoming flagship report *Innovative China: New Drivers of Growth*, the study on land-based transport in Europe-Asia trade, and other studies on China transport and logistics.

Before joining the World Bank, Ms. Liu worked as a student research assistant at the University of Pennsylvania and the University of Hong Kong. She applied advanced geographic information system techniques and big data analysis to urban economics and geography research in an innovative way.

Ms. Liu's current interests are railways, freight and logistics, transport economics, and mega infrastructure projects.

She has a BEng in civil engineering from the University of Hong Kong and a master's degree in city planning from the University of Pennsylvania.

Abbreviations

CRC	China Railway Corporation
CRCC	China Railway Construction Corporation Ltd.
CREC	China Railway Group Ltd.
CRH	China Rail Highspeed
EIRR	economic internal rate of return
EMU	electric multiple unit (trainset)
FIRR	financial internal rate of return
FYP	Five-Year Plan
GDP	gross domestic product
GHG	greenhouse gas
HSR	high-speed rail
JV	joint venture
km	kilometer
kph	kilometer per hour
kWh	kilowatt-hour
MLTRP	Medium- and Long-Term Railway Plan
MOR	Ministry of Railways
MOT	Ministry of Transport
NDRC	National Development and Reform Commission
NRA	National Railway Administration
PDL	passenger dedicated line
pkm	passenger-kilometer
RA	Regional Administration
SASAC	State-Owned Assets Supervision and Administration Commission
VOSL	Value of Statistical Life
VOT	value of time
Y	Chinese yuan

Executive Summary

Since 2008 China has put into operation over 25,000 kilometers (km) of dedicated high-speed railway (HSR) lines, far more than the total high-speed lines operating in the rest of the world. The World Bank has provided financing for some 2,600 km of these lines, beginning in 2006. Since then, the World Bank has evaluated and monitored seven projects, five of which are already in service. This report builds on a report prepared by China Railway Design Corporation, together with analysis and experience gained during the World Bank's work. It summarizes China's experience with HSR and presents key lessons for other countries that may be considering high-speed rail investments.

China was the first country with a gross domestic product (GDP) per capita below US$7,000 to invest in developing an HSR network. China is unique in many ways, including size (9.6 million km²); long distances between North and South, and East and West; the current stage in its economic development (GDP of US$7,590 per capita in 2017); and substantial population density (141 people per km²).[1] China has many large cities with population greater than 500,000, located at distances (between 200 and 500 km) that are well suited for HSR.

In 2008 the first fully HSR line in China was opened, between Beijing and Tianjin, coinciding with the 2008 Beijing Olympic Games. Since then, China has opened 25,162 km of high-speed lines (as of end-2017) with design speeds ranging from 200 to 350 km per hour (kph). It is by far the largest passenger-dedicated HSR network in the world and currently operates over 2,600 pairs of China Rail Highspeed (CRH)[2] trains each day.

The high-speed services represent a radical change in the provision of passenger services by China Railways. Not only have travel times been markedly reduced, but capacity has also significantly expanded. For the first time, passengers on most HSR routes can now "turn up and go," except at peak periods. Over 10 years, the CRH service has carried over 7 billion high-speed passengers, second only to the 11 billion carried by the Japanese Shinkansen over the past 50 years. CRH currently carries 56 percent of the 8.3 million passengers using the China nonurban rail network each day.

The current level of demand, at 1.7 billion passengers per year, confirms the strong need for such service along core corridors and the willingness of many to pay substantially higher fares than charged for conventional intercity trains. The total annual volume carried is already far larger than on the French TGV services and the Japanese Shinkansen services. It will continue to grow rapidly as the many lines under construction are completed and as urban incomes and population in China continue to rise. Traffic on conventional rail services has continued to grow despite diversion to high-speed services, but at a very slow pace (0.5 percent per year). Compared with other leading countries with HSR services, China has achieved a strong start with good traffic densities at an early stage of implementation.

A broad range of travelers of different income levels select the HSR for its short travel time, comfort, convenience, safety, and punctuality. It facilitates labor mobility, family visits, tourism, and expansion of social networks. Nearly half of the passengers travel for business purposes.

By offering a new service quality at a very different price point, China has broadened the range of intercity options, enabling a better matching of supply and demand. This has freed up considerable capacity on conventional trains, on which tickets were formerly very difficult to secure, for lower-income groups who are more price sensitive.

During the past decade, China has accumulated considerable experience in planning, constructing, and operating high-speed lines. This report summarizes key lessons from this experience that may be applicable in other countries.

The first chapter outlines the background to the development of HSR in China and the key role played by the Medium- and Long-Term Railway Plan (MLTRP). This plan, first approved in 2004 with revisions in 2008 and 2016, looks up to 15 years ahead and is complemented by a series of Five-Year Plans, prepared as part of the general planning cycle. These plans are rarely changed once approved. The initial Medium and Long Term Development Plan planned for an HSR network of 12,000 km by 2020. The 2016 revision is now aiming for a network of 30,000 km by 2020, 38,000 km by 2025, and 45,000 km by 2030 (NDRC 2016). The development of a well-analyzed long-term plan, strongly supported by government, provides a clear framework for development of the system.

The lines have been constructed from the start through special-purpose asset construction and management companies. These companies are normally joint ventures between the central and provincial governments. This structure secures the active participation of local government in planning and financing the projects. Cooperation among rail manufacturers, universities, research institutions, laboratories, and engineering centers enables capacity development, rapid technological advancement, and localization of technology.

The second chapter discusses the key choices in service design. Service frequency must balance operating cost and use of line capacity with attractiveness to potential passengers. Most HSR lines have at least an hourly service between 7:00 a.m. and midnight. This level of service requires an average load of 4 million to 6 million passengers per year throughout its route to be operated efficiently. On most lines, the China Railway Corporation (CRC) operates a mixture of express and stopping services. Few services stop at all intermediate stations. The choice of service frequency is matched to the volume of passengers using the station. Line speed is determined by balancing the line's role in the network, market demand, and engineering conditions with investment cost.

Fares are competitive with bus and airfares. Chinese HSR fares are low compared to other countries, which enables HSR to attract passengers from all income groups.

The third chapter analyzes the market for HSR. It gives examples of HSR's ability to attract passengers from other modes (including conventional rail). In corridors in China, HSR typically captures up to half of the conventional rail traffic, most of the intercity bus traffic (except for short distances), and a large share of air traffic up to 800 km. In China, HSR also generates 10–20 percent new trips that were not previously made by any mode.[3] Although half of the trips are made for business purposes, the low fares enable HSR to attract passengers for all trip purposes and from all income groups.

The fourth chapter describes the procedures China has adopted when constructing new lines. One of the most striking lessons for other countries is the speed with which public sector organizations can build high-quality infrastructure when given clear guidance and responsibilities. The Chinese HSR network has been built at an average cost of $17 million to $21 million per km—about two-thirds of the cost in other countries—even though many Chinese lines have a high proportion of their route on viaducts or in tunnels.

Although labor costs are lower in China, a key factor in the lower cost and rapid and efficient HSR construction has been the standardization of designs and procedures. The steady stream of projects has also encouraged the creation of a capable, competitive supply industry. The large HSR investment program, which does not change once approved, has also encouraged the development of innovative and competitive capacity for equipment manufacture and construction and the ability to amortize the capital cost of construction equipment over multiple projects.

HSR project managers have clear responsibilities and delegated authority to carry them out. They typically stay for the full duration of the project, ensuring a clear chain of responsibility for the implementation of the project. Their compensation includes a significant component of incentive compensation related to performance.

The fifth chapter discusses the procedures China has adopted when commissioning new lines and its approach to ensuring operational safety. China manages safety risks throughout the project life cycle by assuring appropriate technology in the design phase, quality construction in the building phase, and thorough inspection and maintenance in the operational phase.

To ensure safe operation, China collects asset condition data through a mix of physical inspection and dynamic testing with instrumented equipment. These data are analyzed centrally to identify maintenance requirements. During operation, a test train is run at the start of each day's operations to check the infrastructure. An instrumented train is run every 10 days to check condition. A four-hour window is provided every night for maintenance.

The sixth chapter explains the financing of the system. As might be expected, the financial picture varies from line to line. Heavily used 350 kph lines with average traffic densities of more than 40 million passengers per year and average revenue per passenger-kilometer (pkm) of Y 0.50 (US$0.074) are able to generate enough ticket revenue to pay for train operations, maintenance, and debt service.

In contrast, many lines in China with traffic density of 10 million to 15 million passengers per year, especially 250 kph lines with average pkm revenue of Y 0.28 (US$0.041), can barely cover train operations and maintenance, and will be unable to contribute toward their debt service costs for many years. These results should not be interpreted as demonstrating that a 350 kph line is inherently more financially viable than a comparable 250 kph line. The main reason for the disparity in financial viability is the pricing policy that has been adopted in China. This issue has been recognized, and greater pricing flexibility is now being allowed.

Options to improve cost coverage for loss-making lines include (i) increasing fares for 250 kph lines where traffic demand permits, (ii) increasing nonfare revenue, and (iii) providing government subsidy. Financial restructuring actions include (i) grouping feeder lines with main lines to pool revenues and costs and (ii) reprofiling principle repayments to shift payments to later years when traffic volumes are greater. Overall, the financial rate of return for the network as it was at end-2015 is estimated at 6 percent,[4] a return on par with the cost of financing of CRC.[5]

The seventh chapter discusses the economic impact of the HSR services. These services provide major benefits to users in terms of reduced travel time, increased service frequencies, greater availability of seats, and improved comfort.

Economic benefits also accrue from reductions in operating cost as users of higher-cost modes such as automobile and air transfer to HSR. These transfers also generally reduce externalities (accidents, highway congestion, and greenhouse gases).[6] Benefits also derive from the deferral of the need to invest in expanding the capacity of other modes as a result of demand transferring to HSR.

Other economic benefits are associated with improved regional connectivity. HSR can contribute to rebalancing growth geographically to reduce poverty and enhance inclusiveness.

Overall, the economic results appear positive, even at this early stage. The economic rate of return of the network as it was in 2015 is estimated at 8 percent, well above the opportunity cost of capital adopted in China and most other countries for such major long-term infrastructure investments. There is thus a reason to be optimistic about the long-term economic viability of the major trunk railways of the HSR program in China.

How much of this experience is replicable and potentially instructive for other countries considering investment in HSR? Potential lessons and replicable practices include

- A well-analyzed Long-Term Plan, supported by government, with minimal changes once approved;
- Standardization of designs;
- Competitive supply industry;
- Partnering with local government;
- Project management structure with clear responsibilities and decision-making authority, managers who stay for the duration of the project, and significant incentive compensation for managers;
- Safety system that identifies and manages risk during all project phases;
- Service with high punctuality, frequency, and speed;
- Value of good connectivity with conventional rail and urban transport;
- High-volume, medium-distance markets;
- Pricing that is affordable and competitive with other modes, and finds the "sweet spot" that maximizes revenue while not substantially discouraging ridership; and
- Offering a range of services (high speed and conventional) at different price points to meet different passenger needs.

NOTES

1. The Central and Eastern Provinces are particularly dense, with average population of 420 people per km², about the same as the Netherlands.
2. In this report, HSR refers to the high-speed network—that is, lines on which services can travel at over 200 kph. This network includes both the dedicated new passenger lines with a design speed of 200 kph or above and the new passenger-freight lines with a maximum design speed of 200 kph. CRH refers to the train services that operate over these lines; some of these trains also continue on upgraded conventional lines. A similar situation occurs in France, where the TGV trains operate on both the high-speed network (LGV) and connecting sections of the conventional network.
3. The generation of new traffic is discussed in chapter 3 in the section titled "New Traffic."
4. Assuming inflation of 2 percent per year.
5. Assuming inflation of 2 percent per year.
6. However, GHG savings during operation need to be balanced against GHG generated during construction, either directly or through the GHG embedded in construction materials such as cement and steel.

REFERENCE

NDRC (National Development and Reform Commission). 2016. "Mid- and Long-Term Railway Network Plan." National Development and Reform Commission of the People's Republic of China, Beijing.

1 Growth of High-Speed Rail in China

One of the most striking achievements of the Chinese high-speed rail (HSR) program is the speed with which it has been developed and implemented. How has this been achieved, and is it replicable elsewhere?

RAIL INDUSTRY STRUCTURE

Before 2013 almost all public railways were operated and regulated by the Ministry of Railways (MOR). Often termed "the last fortress of China's planned economy," the MOR had wide-ranging powers that were important in the introduction and localization of key HSR technology and in rapid infrastructure construction.

However, this model combining sector administration with commercial activities became increasingly incompatible with the establishment of the modern enterprise system in China and the proposed reforms of the Chinese railway system. Consequently, in 2013 MOR was split into the National Railway Administration (NRA) and the China Railway Corporation (CRC) (see figure 1.1).

The NRA is the bureau within the Ministry of Transport (MOT) responsible for the management and administration of the rail sector as a whole,[1] including

- Laws and regulations governing the sector;
- Formulation and implementation of railway technical standards;
- Management of railway safety, including the licensing of participants and investigation of railway accidents;
- Regulation of rail transport and construction;
- Supervision of service quality and public service obligations undertaken by railway enterprises; and
- Monitoring and analysis of railway operations and the rail industry.

FIGURE 1.1

Structure of China's high-speed rail sector

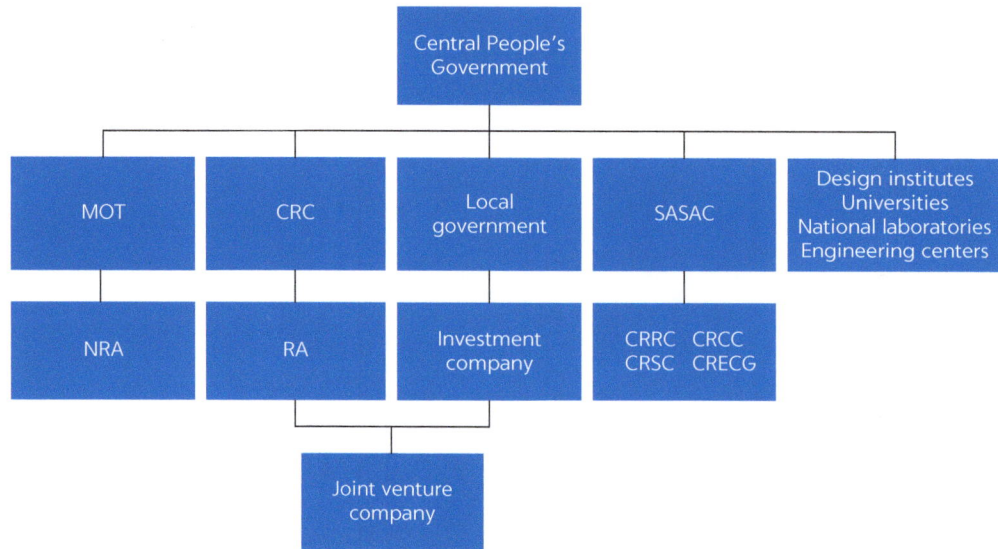

Note: CRC = China Railway Corporation; CRCC = China Railway Construction Corporation; CRECG = China Railway Engineering Corporation; CRRC = China Railway Rolling Stock Corporation; CRSC = China Railway Signal & Communication Corporation; MOT = Ministry of Transport; NRA = National Railway Administration; RA = Regional Administration; SASAC = State-Owned Assets Supervision and Administration Commission.

CRC is a 100 percent state-owned enterprise with its shares held by the Ministry of Finance. It is responsible for the management and safety of almost all the 127,000 kilometer (km) public network, including

- The unified dispatching and control of railway transport;
- Operation and management of passenger and freight transport services;
- Public-benefit transport;
- The railway construction investment plan and national railway construction and financing arrangements in conjunction with the National Development and Reform Commission (NDRC); and
- Preparatory work for and subsequent management of construction projects.

CRC includes several subsidiary companies, of which the most important are the 18 Regional Administrations (RAs). The RAs maintain the rail network and provide train services. Nevertheless, operational and overall construction management of the rail network remains highly centralized, which has been a key factor in achieving such a rapid development of HSR.

The railway sector also includes a complete industrial chain of engineering construction and equipment manufacturing entities, many of which are state-owned enterprises, under the supervision of the State-Owned Assets Supervision and Administration Commission (SASAC). Design institutes and university rail programs are important players in sector development.

HSR SUBSECTOR STRUCTURE

The HSR infrastructure has been built using primarily a joint venture (JV) model. The JV shareholders are typically the central government and provincial government. Some projects also involve third parties such as other nonrailway state-owned enterprises or private companies. The central government is represented by CRC, whereas many provinces have established railway investment companies to hold their ownership interests. The overall financial structure is typically 50 percent equity and 50 percent debt. Each JV partner contributes equity, with the provincial government often making its contribution in the form of land. The JV raises the rest of the financing from loans and other debt.

Although the HSR infrastructure is the property of the JV, most JVs usually do not manage the rail services. Instead, the JV contracts with the local RA completely or partially for

- Operational management, including train operation and train control;
- Infrastructure and equipment management;
- Rolling stock management;
- Safety management;
- Revenue management; and
- Management of railway land use, including patrolling and maintenance of boundaries.

HSR PLANNING

A key development in China was the development and approval in 2004 of a Medium- and Long-Term Railway Plan (MLTRP) covering freight and passenger network development to 2020, including the construction of an HSR network. The original MLTRP has since been updated twice and extended to 2030. It is implemented through a series of Five-Year Railway Development Plans (FYPs) setting out the projects to be undertaken in each five-year cycle (currently 2016–20). The FYP is consistent with the MLTRP while also ensuring the coordination of the national railway development with other sectors of the economy for each five-year cycle.[2] The railway plans also reflect higher-level plans such as the National Economy and Social Development Plan and the Comprehensive Transportation System Plan.

The MLTRP and FYP have been jointly prepared by the NDRC, MOT, and CRC (or their equivalents at the time). The plans are based on a detailed analytical process involving basic investigations, data collection, project research, and screening of the major projects included in the plan, as well as extensive external consultation and review by an expert advisory committee.

The MLTRP was the first industry plan of its type to be approved by the State Council.[3] After State Council approval, the MLTRP is jointly issued by NDRC, MOT, and CRC. Thus, the MLTRP and FYP have the authority of the highest level of government.

Once the plan is released, it cannot be subsequently modified. The State Council departments provide active support and develop and refine the supporting policies. Provinces and municipalities also formulate provincial and municipal railway plans, which are coordinated with national planning and provide support as required.

In summary, a continuing strong commitment from the top level of government, combined with the strong capacity of the implementing agency, has been a major factor in achieving the 2004 planning goals. This unwavering support for the plan, once issued, may be a unique feature of the Chinese political system and difficult to replicate elsewhere.

HSR NETWORK DEVELOPMENT

Prior to the MLTRP, a considerable amount of work had been done to develop and test HSR infrastructure and rolling stock (box 1.1). China Railways had undertaken a series of "speed-up" campaigns for the passenger services. The sixth of these, completed in April 2007, saw the introduction of China Rail Highspeed (CRH)[4] services. It included improved schedules and track (about 6,000 km or so was upgraded) on several busy corridors and the introduction of a new generation of trains able to operate at a top speed of 250 km per hour (kph). At that time, however, most CRH trains still had to share heavily used tracks with freight trains, resulting in moderate station-to-station speeds, even if top speed had markedly improved.[5]

The 2004 MLTRP was the first time an HSR network was proposed. At that time, freight volume was growing rapidly at about 7.5 percent per year and was straining network capacity. Low speed of the existing railway limited the railway's competitiveness in passenger transport. The plan target was that, by 2020, the national railway infrastructure would grow to 100,000 route-km, of which 12,000 km would be high speed (HSR).[6]

The high-speed passenger dedicated lines (PDLs) would form four horizontal and four vertical corridors (map 1.1) linking all major cities. Except for the Hangzhou–Shenzhen corridor, all the main corridors paralleled existing conventional lines, which were either at or approaching capacity. It was difficult to purchase tickets at short notice, and long-distance trips were given priority over short-distance ones. The plan was that all long-distance passenger traffic would transfer to the new services, leaving only a limited number of local services on the existing lines and thus providing a large increment of capacity for expanded freight services.

BOX 1.1

Maglev or conventional track?

Initially, China faced a technology choice between conventional track and maglev. A 30-kilometer (km) trial maglev project was constructed linking Pudong Airport in Shanghai to the then terminus of the Metro network. It started operation in 2002. Although technically successful, it had a very high capital cost. Little technology was available on a commercial scale, and maglev was incompatible with the existing railway. China thus decided to stay with conventional rail technology adapted for high-speed rail (HSR).

Two sections of HSR line (over 500 km in total) were opened in 2003 and 2006 as testing grounds for various aspects of HSR construction, and a special group was established to adapt international technology and develop integrated technical systems (for example, power, signaling) for HSR in China.

These efforts were supported by the decision in 2008 to make China as self-sufficient as possible in HSR technology by mobilizing research and development resources on a massive scale to establish China's own systems and standards. The size of the HSR program subsequently enabled China to climb the learning curve, achieve significant economies of scale, and make it worthwhile to invest in a wide-ranging research and development program covering all aspects of engineering, operation, and management. Few countries outside China are large enough to have similar programs.

MAP 1.1
Planned high-speed rail corridors

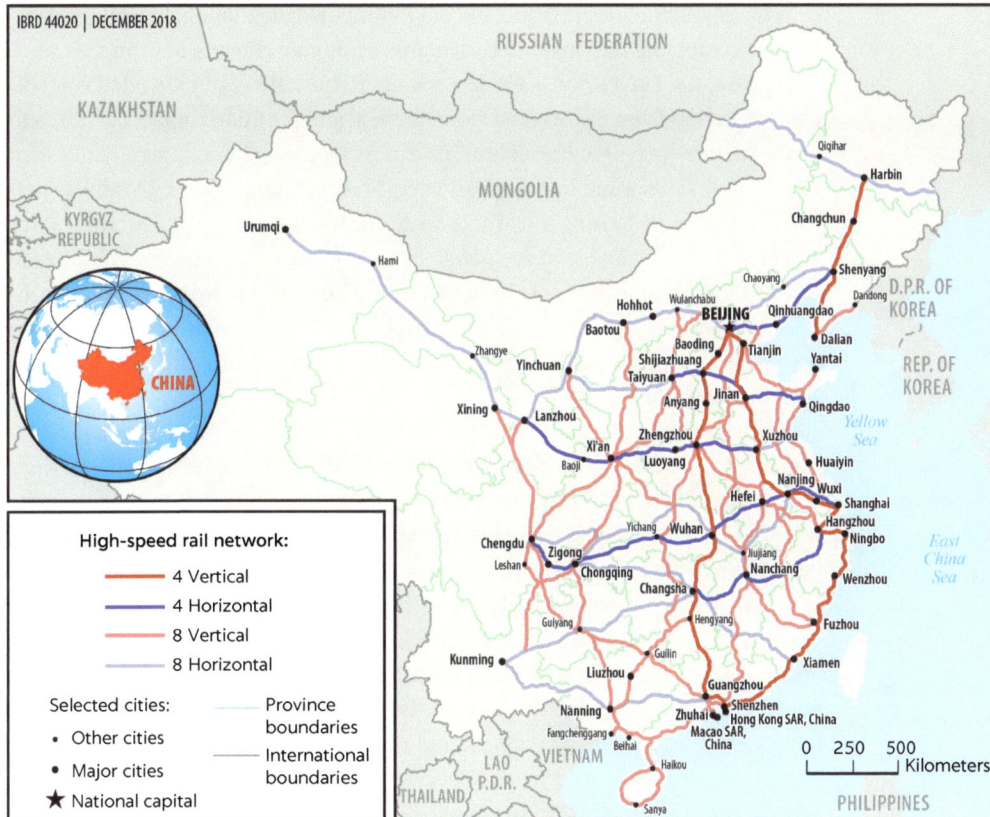

The MLTRP also included three regional intercity networks (now known as "rapid-rail") for (i) the Bohai Sea ring (Tianjin, Beijing, Hebei province); (ii) the Yangtze River Delta (Shanghai, 16 cities in central and eastern Jiangsu and Zhejiang provinces); and (iii) the Pearl River Delta (central and southern Guangdong province), covering the major cities and towns in each area. These lines would provide services for short- and medium-distance passengers in these regions with metro-like frequency.

By 2008, with the rapid development of the national economy, the importance of the railway had increased and local and regional governments were keen to invest to accelerate the 2004 program. This coincided with the global financial crisis, and the central government wished to provide an economic stimulus to minimize its impact in China. Additional projects were proposed, and the MLTRP was revised with 2020 development targets of 120,000 km of national railway route-km, nine regional intercity networks, and 16,000 km of PDL.

In August 2008, the first of the new generation of HSR lines started operating when the Beijing–Tianjin intercity HSR line opened, with a maximum speed of 350 kph and an average station-to-station speed of 240 kph. It combined fully dedicated tracks, mostly on viaduct, with electric multiple units (EMUs) and quickly established itself as a competitive form of transport, carrying over 16 million passengers in its first full year of operation.

In 2009, the first major long-distance route started operating between Guangzhou and Wuhan via Changsha. By December 2012, both the 1,318 km Beijing–Shanghai line and the 2,105 km Beijing–Guangzhou line had been completed, connecting the three most dynamic economic clusters in China.

In 2016, the MLTRP was further revised. The 2016 plan expanded the network structure from the original "four vertical and four horizontal" corridors to "eight vertical and eight horizontal" corridors (see map 1.1), supplemented with more regional links and intercity railways. The 2020 target is now a railway network reaching 150,000 km, including 30,000 km of HSR reaching over 80 percent of large and medium-sized cities.[7] By 2025, the network would reach 175,000 km, including 38,000 km of HSR. The HSR network will then connect almost all large and medium-size cities. It will create travel times of 1.0–4.0 hours between the large and medium-sized cities and 0.5–2.0 hours around the regional centers.

Since then, the HSR network has continued to expand to reach over 25,000 route-km as of end-2017. (See figure 1.2, which also includes mixed-use lines operating at 200 kph.) The Chinese network now encompasses 66 percent of the world's total HSR lines—twice the total of all other countries. Map 1.2 shows the geographical development of the network between 2008 and 2017.

Growth in the planned network has thus been accompanied by a change in the underlying rationale. The original objective was to provide additional capacity for an overloaded network and enable a much-improved passenger service to be developed to provide efficient medium-distance transport. The emphasis now is more on improving regional and provincial connectivity to support economic development and urbanization. However, the basic elements have remained the same, thus preserving the continuity and consistency of the plan and allowing its rapid development in an orderly manner.

FIGURE 1.2

Length of China's high-speed rail network, 2008–17

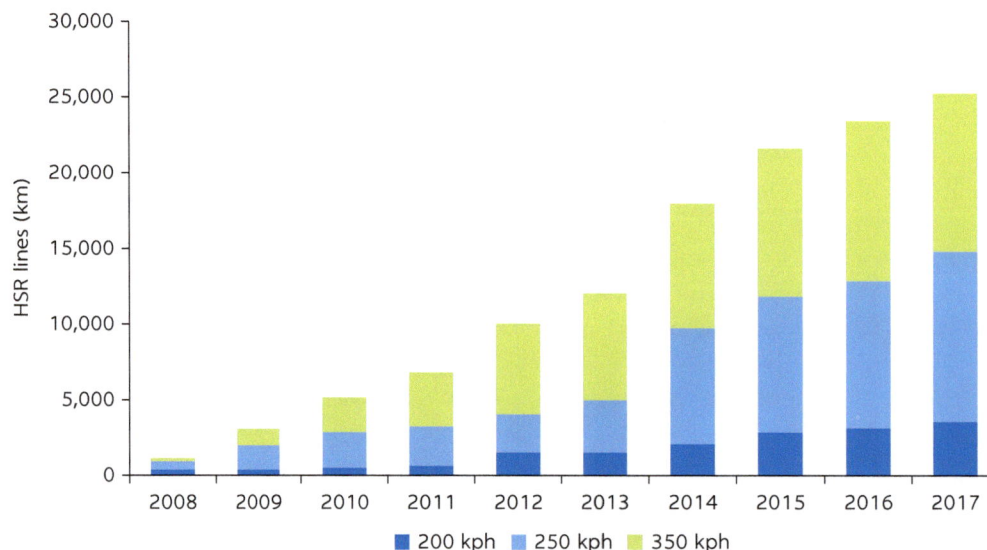

Source: Based on data from China Railway Yearbooks 2008–17.
Note: HSR = high-speed rail; km = kilometer; kph = km per hour.

MAP 1.2

Growth of China's high-speed rail network, 2008–17

a. High-speed rail network, 2008

b. High-speed rail network, 2009

continued

MAP 1.2, *continued*

c. High-speed rail network, 2010

d. High-speed rail network, 2011

continued

MAP 1.2, *continued*

e. High-speed rail network, 2012

IBRD 44051 | DECEMBER 2018

f. High-speed rail network, 2013

IBRD 44052 | DECEMBER 2018

continued

MAP 1.2, *continued*

g. High-speed rail network, 2014

h. High-speed rail network, 2015

continued

MAP 1.2, *continued*

i. High-speed rail network, 2016

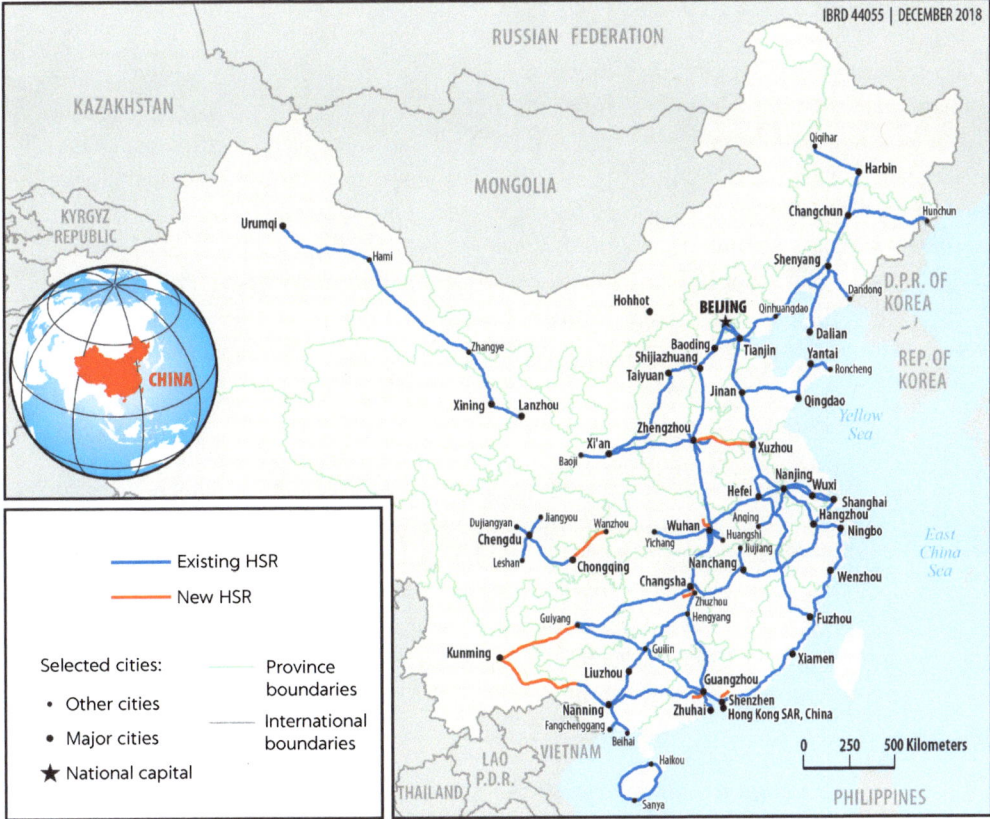

j. High-speed rail network, 2017

Note: HSR = high-speed rail.

BOX 1.2

Research and development capacity

China has developed a broad "ecosystem" of universities and research organizations that work with suppliers to deliver improved products. For example, to develop the "Fuxing" 350 kph trainset, in 2008 the Ministry of Science and Technology and the former Ministry of Railways jointly signed a Cooperation Agreement of China High-Speed Train Independent Innovation Joint Action Plan. This plan brings together six large-scale central enterprises, 25 key universities, 11 first-class scientific research institutes, 51 national laboratories and engineering centers, and a scientific and technological team composed of 68 academicians, 500 professors, and over 10 thousand engineers and technicians. This collaboration allowed China to introduce, digest, absorb, and reinnovate foreign advanced electric multiple unit technology in a short period of time to create a successful product.

To deliver a program of this scale, China needed to develop a technological base for both infrastructure components and rolling stock (box 1.2). Although early high-speed trainsets were imported or built under technology transfer agreements with European and Japanese suppliers, China rapidly adapted and improved the designs for local use. China has worked with the International Railway Union (UIC) to develop international standards for HSR equipment, and its technology is compliant with these standards.

CURRENT NETWORK

Most major metropolitan regions in China are now either connected or in the process of being connected to lines with a maximum speed of 200 kph or above.

The new HSR lines are of three general types. Trunk lines are passenger-only lines designed to operate at a maximum speed of 350 kph. These lines operate at higher average station-to-station speeds than most of their international counterparts,[8] with the proviso that many stations are located outside central areas and thus require additional connection time to and from central areas. Secondary main lines and regional connectors are designed with a maximum speed of 250 kph. Other intercity lines are designed with a maximum speed of 200 kph. Some of these are passenger-only whereas others are designed to carry both passengers and express freight such as container services.

Many opportunities have developed to connect cities through services over a combination of lines, with, for example, direct trains between Beijing and Xi'an via Zhengzhou. Networking is an important feature of Chinese HSR. North–south vertical lines and east–west horizontal lines provide the basic network skeleton, supplemented with regional and intercity railway lines.

Each HSR line thus creates flows for other lines. For example, 24 percent of the passengers traveling on the Beijing–Shanghai line in 2016 were traveling to and from stations that were not on the line itself but on connecting lines. Another example is the Zhengzhou–Xi'an line, which until 2012 was an isolated line, serving only passengers between Zhengzhou and Xi'an. After it was connected to the Beijing–Guangzhou HSR in 2013, passenger volume increased by 43 percent and passenger-km by 72 percent. By 2016, about half the

Highlights

Key factors contributing to the rapid implementation of an HSR network in China include

- Development of a well-analyzed Long-Term Plan that provides a clear and consistent framework for action;
- Strong government support for the implementation of the Long-Term Plan;
- Five-Year Plans that detail the implementation of the Long-Term Plan, setting out the work program for each plan period; once decided, these plans are rarely changed, providing a clear framework within which local governments and the construction/supply industry can plan with confidence;
- Minimal changes to individual project plans once they are approved;
- Joint venture structure ensuring active participation of provincial and local governments in the planning and financing of the projects; and
- Cooperation among rail manufacturers, universities, research institutions, laboratories, and engineering centers allowing for rapid technological advancement and localization of technology.

Zhengzhou–Xi'an HSR passengers were traveling to and from stations off the line itself.

A major feature of the HSR network has been the expansion of coverage which has improved the accessibility of different regions and cities. As megacities form across the country, surrounded by a cluster of provincial cities, the HSR network aims to link all cities of 0.5 million or more within one to four hours to a megacity, and to create a traffic circle of under two hours for each of the provincial clusters.

NOTES

1. Excludes dedicated industrial lines serving mines, forestry, and industries, which are managed and administered by the corporations that own them.
2. China's planning system comprises three levels and three types of plan. Plans are prepared at the state, provincial, and county levels. They are then divided by object and functional category into general plans, special plans, and regional plans.
3. The highest level of government in China.
4. CRH refers to the services and the trainsets that can operate on both conventional and dedicated high-speed lines.
5. With a 10-hour trip, the average speed between Beijing and Shanghai had improved to about 132 kph.
6. Known as passenger dedicated lines (PDLs) until the 2016 revision to the MLTRP.
7. Provincial capitals and cities with over half a million people.
8. The fastest services between Beijing and Zhengzhou (693 km) and between Beijing and Shanghai (1,318 km) average 289 kph and 275 kph, respectively. The fastest service between Paris and Marseilles (783 km) averages 253 kph.

2 Service Design

CURRENT SERVICE LEVELS

In early 2018, China Railway Corporation (CRC) operated over 2,600 pairs of China Rail Highspeed (CRH) trains per day, 68 percent of the total trains operated on the entire rail network. This number included over 100 CRH pairs daily on most of the Beijing–Shanghai line and over 80 CRH pairs on the Beijing–Guangzhou line. All high-speed rail (HSR) and 200-kilometer-per-hour (kph) trains are operated with electric multiple unit (EMU) trains consisting of 8 or 16 carriages, with the train capacity ranging from 494 seats to 1,299 seats. According to current CRC train schedules, 70 to 130 pairs of HSR trains are operated daily on busy routes, with up to eight pairs of trains per hour operated during peak hours. Traffic density on such routes is estimated at 60 million to 70 million passengers. On medium-density routes, 40 to 50 pairs of trains are operated daily.

Two types of services are generally provided on any given line. Express trains stop only at major cities whereas other trains stop at some, but rarely all, intermediate stations. Direct services between two intermediate stations can thus be infrequent, although trips can be made indirectly by changing at a larger station.

Most services operate intensively, typically with hourly or half-hourly intervals between 7:00 a.m. and midnight (table 2.1), normally with 16-car sets on the main lines and 8-car sets on the secondary lines. Average occupancy (passenger-km/seat-km) over the network is 70–75 percent.

In 2007, CRH services totaled about 40 million train-km per year, all on conventional "speeded-up" lines. By 2017, this total had increased to over 1 billion train-km per year, almost all of which was on dedicated lines with a maximum design speed of 250 kph or more (map 2.1).

SERVICE FREQUENCY, CAPACITY, AND MARKET SIZE

Service frequency is an important aspect of service design, balancing operating cost and use of line capacity with attractiveness to potential passengers.

21

TABLE 2.1 Selected high-speed rail service patterns, August 2018

SECTION	FIRST DEPARTURE	LAST ARRIVAL	SERVICES/DAY[a]
Intercity lines			
Beijing–Tianjin	06:46	23:25	100
Changchun–Jilin	05:45	23:01	69
Shanghai–Nanjing	05:48	23:30	227[b]
Guangzhou–Shenzhen	06:00	23:37	191[b]
Chengdu–Chongqing	06:39	23:29	78
Long-distance lines			
Beijing–Shanghai	06:39	23:39	44
Wuhan–Guangzhou	06:22	23:44	54
Zhengzhou–Xi'an	05:56	22:52	32
Wenzhou–Fuzhou	07:10	22:24	31

a. Per direction; some lines also have services to/from intermediate points.
b. Two lines.

MAP 2.1

Speed of China's existing high-speed rail network

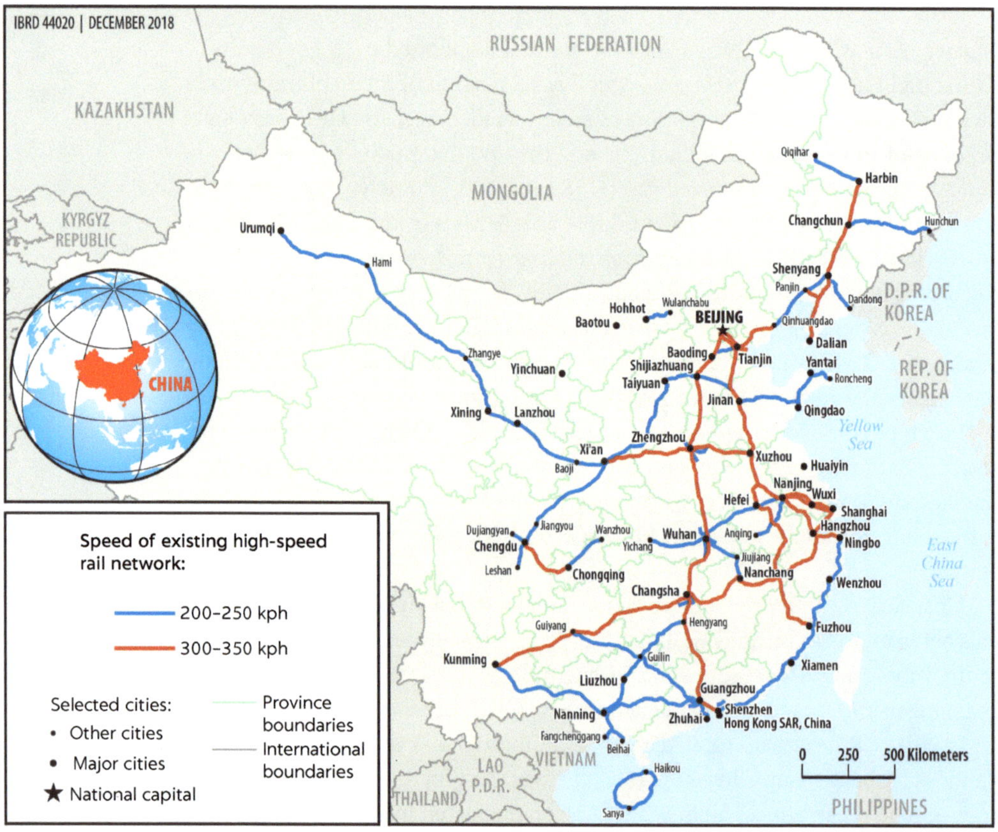

Note: kph = kilometers per hour.

Higher frequencies provide greater choice for passengers who can schedule trips more flexibly. However, service frequency needs to be supported by a sufficiently large passenger flow. Otherwise many seats are wasted and idle, the occupancy is reduced, and the unit operating cost is increased. There thus needs to be a reasonable match between service frequency and passenger demand and a balance between service levels and operational benefits.

China operates two types of HSR services: regional intercity services and long-distance services. These two services have different service characteristics and frequencies.

The regional intercity railways are medium- and short-distance HSRs built in densely populated urban agglomerations or city belts to connect major towns and economic nodes. They operate with high service frequencies. For example, the intercity railway between Beijing and Tianjin, each with a population of more than 15 million, has a travel time of about 35 minutes. Daily service frequencies have increased from 47 pairs at its opening to 100 pairs currently, with service intervals of under 10 minutes at peak times and 25 minutes in the off-peak. Many other city pairs have service frequencies of 60 pairs per day or more, equivalent to a service of four trains per hour in each direction (table 2.1).

Regional intercity railways need to adopt high service frequency with appropriate train sizes to ensure market competitiveness. Even if passenger traffic is small at the beginning of operation, a minimum service frequency should be guaranteed; this minimum can be determined only by analysis of the transport market (box 2.1). Chinese experience is that the service interval should not exceed 30 minutes during peak periods and one hour in off-peak periods.

Long-distance lines must accommodate a mix of long-distance and short-distance trains and be organized to connect and transfer passengers to/from intersecting lines. For example, the Beijing–Shanghai line connects 11 cities with populations of 1 million or more over 1,318 km. Currently there are 248 pairs of trains running on all or part of the line every day; of those trains only 44 run the entire distance. On any one section, the total number of timetabled trains varies between 110 pairs and 144 pairs and the end-to-end trains thus represent only about 30–40 percent of the total services.

There are 23 stations on the Beijing–Shanghai HSR. The fastest train stops at 2 stations in the middle and takes four hours and 24 minutes; the slowest train stops at 10 stations and takes six hours and 12 minutes. The more stops each service has the higher the service frequency for the intermediate stops but the greater the travel time for everyone on board. The stopping plan thus also needs to be matched with the traffic volume at each station. CRC has evolved the stopping plans over time in response to experience and customer feedback.

| BOX 2.1 |

Implications for market size

With an hourly service from 7:00 a.m. to 11:00 p.m. and the minimum eight-car train capacity of 494 seats, the lowest seat capacity offered on a high-speed rail service is approximately 6 million seats per year. Applying a reasonable load factor (for example, 70 percent) would indicate a minimum market size of 4 million passengers per year to make good use of the capacity.

CHOOSING THE SPEED OF HSR

The design speed of an HSR line is the maximum running speed of an EMU based on the design standards for the line. It is the lower of the infrastructure design speed and the equipment design speed. The operating speed is restricted by the design speed, and the maximum practical operating speed of EMU is chosen by considering factors such as operating cost, unit energy consumption, safety redundancy, noise, and vibration. The infrastructure is difficult to change once it has been built, but the equipment can be upgraded by technical improvements.

TABLE 2.2 Classification of HSR lines

CLASSIFICATION	DESIGN SPEED (kph)	OPERATION SPEED (kph)	APPLICABILITY	TECHNICAL STANDARDS
300–350 kph	350	300–350	Main line	Code for Design of High-Speed Railway
200–250 kph	250	200–250	Regional connector	Code for Design of High-Speed Railway
	200	200	Intercity rail	Code for Design of Intercity Railway

Note: HSR = high-speed rail; kph = kilometers per hour.

At present in China the HSR lines designed for 350 kph are operated at 300 or 350 kph. The HSR lines designed for 250 kph are operated at 200 or 250 kph. The HSR lines designed for 200 kph are operated at 200 kph. The HSR in China can thus be divided into two groups: 300–350 kph and 200–250 kph. By the end of 2017, the length of 300–350 kph lines was about 10,000 km, and the length of 200–250 kph lines was about 15,000 km (table 2.2 and map 2.1).

The functional classification of a line is determined by the economic level and population size of the region, the number and size of the connected towns, the characteristics of the passenger flow in the corridor, and the role it plays in the railway network. HSR projects within the "eight vertical and eight horizontal HSR corridors"—which serve densely populated corridors, have a developed economy, carry a large proportion of long-distance traffic, and connect provincial capitals and megacities—generally adopt 350 kph. Regional connecting lines generally adopt 250 kph. Intercity rails, which mainly connect prefecture-level cities, with a large proportion of their passenger traffic in the middle to short distance and a lesser role in the network, usually adopt 200 kph.

Although the functional classifications are observed, factors such as market competition, engineering conditions, investment benefit, and the transport organization plan are also considered for any individual line. Higher speed helps to save travel time, improve rolling stock productivity, and improve the competitiveness of the high-speed rail. Higher speed also means a corresponding increase in operating costs and fares. Thus, the speed and fare combination needs to be selected according to the specific analysis of the transportation market.

No matter what speed standard is adopted, operation safety must be guaranteed. Lowering speed is sometimes taken as a security measure, so safety may also affect decisions about speed.

The design speed of any given HSR line should also be compatible with the transport organization plan. For example, the speed standard should match adjoining lines when the number of interlining trains is large. There is also little benefit to adopting higher speed standards for lines going only a short distance or with many closely spaced stations. In practice, the choice of speed is thus a balance between not only technical and economic factors but also the overall network management.

From an engineering perspective, the design speed for a given line should consider the terrain, geomorphology, and geological conditions along the line. Once the civil works have been constructed, it is difficult to reconstruct to a higher standard. Sometimes, therefore, a higher standard is adopted at the outset to permit a future speed increase. Some HSR lines with a general design speed of 350 kph may also have sections with lower design speeds (for example, with smaller horizontal curves in urban areas to reduce land acquisition and demolition and save construction costs).

OPERATIONAL MANAGEMENT

Operational management of an interconnected HSR network is clearly more complex than managing a single point-to-point line. This challenge has been approached in China by keeping a single point of overall control exercised by CRC. Whereas CRC monitors and coordinates the overall operations, however, the individual Regional Administrations (RAs) are responsible for controlling the physical operations within their jurisdictions.

From the user's viewpoint, there is a uniform product with uniform ticketing. The three types of service (G, D, and C) provide a consistent service throughout the network. The ticketing system allows passengers to purchase, cancel, and change tickets for any train in the HSR network at any time, using physical, telephone, and Internet channels.

From the operator's viewpoint, integrated management of the network provides easier opportunities to provide through services and allow indirect services via major hubs. It also provides a degree of operational flexibility if line sections are unusable. It improves equipment utilization, and equipment maintenance can be standardized with maintenance facilities shared between lines. For example, the 48 EMU depots in the network have been organized into seven groups, with one depot in each group providing major maintenance and the others concentrating on routine and periodic maintenance.

HSR FARE STRUCTURE

In China, prices of certain goods and services may be subject to government guidance under the Price Law, and railway transport has historically been subject to this law. HSR fares were therefore guided by the State Council until 2016.

HSR prices were historically determined according to the speed level, with two bands for 200–250 kph and 300–350 kph:

- The published fare of 200–250 kph EMU trains is set by CRC although an RA can discount such fares if it chooses, according to market conditions.
- The 300–350 kph EMU trains are currently implementing the trial pricing policy for new products, in which the price is based on the public purchasing power and market supply.

HSR fares were unchanged from 2007 to 2016, apart from a 5 percent reduction in 2011 (table 2.3). Discounts are available for children, students, and other

TABLE 2.3 China's high-speed rail fares, 2011–16

SPEED (kph)	FIRST CLASS	SECOND CLASS
	Fare (Y/pkm)	
300–350	0.74	0.46
200–250	0.35[a]	0.29
	Fare (US$/pkm @ Y 6.70 = US$1.00)	
300–350	0.110	0.069
200–250	0.052	0.043

Note: kph = kilometers per hour; pkm = passenger-kilometer; Y = Chinese yuan.
a. First class fares for 200 kph services can reach as low as Y 0.30/km (US$0.045/km) (almost equal to the cost of second class on new 250 kph track).

target groups. Distance discounts are also applicable to the 350 kph fares, with up to a 20 percent discount for trips over 2,000 km.

This policy has kept HSR prices at a relatively low level for a long time (they are about one-fourth of the base fares applied in most other HSR countries[1]) and allowed the services to be affordable to a large part of the population. It has, however, two significant drawbacks:

1. **Lack of flexibility**: Because HSR fares are only linked to train speed, they are relatively fixed and do not reflect changes in market demand, such as time of day or day of week, the different income levels in different parts of the country, or the differing competition from other modes. As a result, it is difficult to use price adjustments to balance passenger demand and available capacity.[2]

2. **Cost recovery**: The relatively low fares reduce operating income and returns on investment, and it is thus difficult to mobilize private investment in the sector. Since the EMU services began in 2007, per capita disposable income of Chinese urban residents has risen from Y 14,000 (US$2,100) to nearly Y 34,000 (US$5,100), but fares have been almost unchanged.

HSR fares are very competitive with other modes in markets where the door-to-door travel time is also competitive. HSR fares are lower than both aviation—about Y 0.75 per passenger-km (US$0.11/pkm) with shorter trips a bit more expensive—and buses—about Y 0.30/pkm (US$0.044/pkm), with sleeper buses slightly more expensive. The lower-speed lines are thus very price-competitive with bus whereas the higher-speed lines are generally cheaper than air except where heavily discounted air fares are offered (figure 2.1).

The conventional service fares are only Y 0.06/pkm (US$0.009/pkm), and the soft seat price is Y 0.12/pkm (US$0.018/pkm), just one-fourth or less of a 350 kph ticket. These services remain in demand. Many complaints about the high fares arose from existing rail passengers, where cheaper conventional rail services were replaced wholly or partially by HSR.

The fare structure was also criticized for being inflexible and preventing the use of prices to modulate demand in peak periods and fill empty seats in low

FIGURE 2.1

High-speed rail fares compared to bus and air

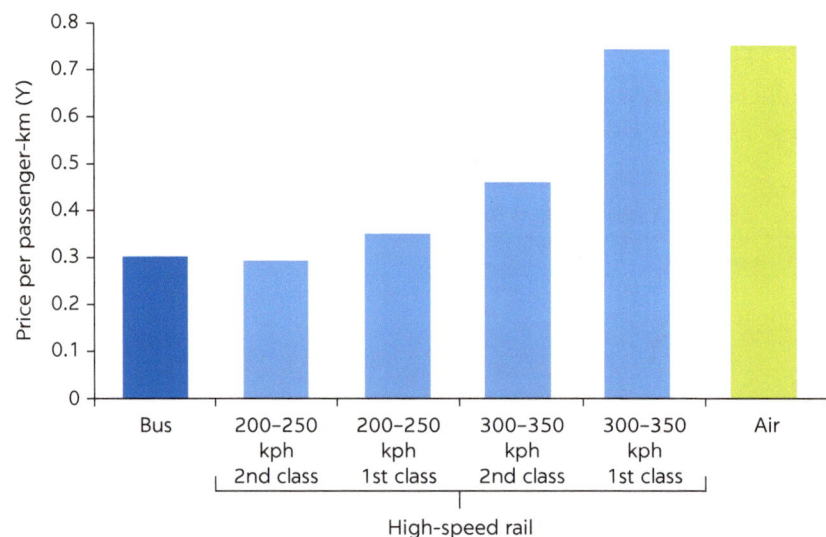

Note: The bus and airfares shown are estimated averages. km = kilometers; kph = km per hour; Y = Chinese yuan.

demand periods (see, for example, Scales, Ollivier, and Amos 2011). In 2016, the central government decided to delegate the pricing power of railway service to CRC, and allow CRC more flexibility in the pricing of HSR, based on the type of service, passenger demand, and local purchasing power.

Since the delegation of the pricing power of HSR to CRC, the price of many existing 200–250 kph lines has changed from the guided price. The first major fare adjustment took place on the coastal line. In April 2017, the Coastal HSR increased its prices by up to 60 percent and 20 percent for first- and second-class travel, respectively. The impact on demand is understood to have been slight, but the line is in an economically developed area and the revised fares are still competitive with competing modes. In another change, CRC has also recently announced discounts on six 200–250 kph services. For HSR lines opened in or after 2016, the price was determined without direct reference to the guided price but was based on the public purchasing power and market supply.

The reform of the HSR pricing mechanism in January 2016 also had an impact on civil aviation, whose pricing mechanism was also reformed in November 2016. Airlines are now allowed to determine the fare for routes shorter than 800 km and routes longer than 800 km that compete with HSR. Thus, as the economy matures and transport capacity increases, the government is gradually loosening its grip on transport prices and letting the market play a bigger role in resource allocation. This should lead to greater resource efficiency over time.

PUNCTUALITY AND RELIABILITY

With strong operational capacity and infrastructure and facilities in good condition, China's HSR service has a good record of punctuality and reliability. The punctuality rate of HSR service in China is over 98 percent for departures and over 95 percent for arrivals. "Fuxing trains," the flagship express service with the newest CRH models on 300–350 kph bulk lines, have even better punctuality—99 percent and 98 percent for departures and arrivals, respectively.

COMBINING THE HSR AND CONVENTIONAL RAIL NETWORKS

The China rail network has many examples of high-speed and normal-speed trains, as well as passenger trains and freight trains, sharing tracks. After six major speed increases, many of the conventional main lines can operate EMUs at 200 kph and some EMU services (for example, Beijing–Northeast China) currently run over a combination of conventional and HSR lines.

Some of the earlier HSR projects were designed with a speed of 200–250 kph and were intended for mixed use (EMU passenger and locomotive-hauled freight). Most did not operate freight trains but some (for example, Shijiazhuang to Taiyuan) are used by locomotive-hauled passenger trains.

The principle followed in China at present is that 250 kph trains can operate on HSR lines built for 300–350 kph; locomotive-hauled passenger trains with speed of 160 kph can operate on HSR lines built for 200–250 kph. Conversely, high-speed EMU trains should operate at no more than 160 kph when running on conventional railways (table 2.4).[3] This adaptability has provided greater operational flexibility and improved service to passengers.

TABLE 2.4 **Line and rolling stock correspondence**

LINE CLASSIFICATION		ROLLING STOCK
High-speed lines	300–350 kph	EMUs operating at or above 250 kph
	200–250 kph	EMUs operating at 160 to 250 kph; conventional trains operating at 160 kph
Conventional lines		Conventional trains; EMUs operating at or below 160 kph

Note: EMU = electric multiple unit; kph = kilometers per hour.

Highlights

- Service frequency must balance operating cost and use of line capacity with attractiveness to potential passengers. Most HSR lines have at least hourly service between 7:00 a.m. and midnight, which requires an average load of 4 million to 6 million passengers per year throughout its route to be operated efficiently.
- On most lines, CRC operates a mixture of express and stopping services. Few services stop at all intermediate stations. The choice of service frequency is matched to the volume of passengers using the station.
- Line speed is determined by balancing the line's role in the network, market demand, and engineering conditions with investment cost.
- Fares are competitive with bus and airfares. Chinese fares are low compared to those in other countries.
- Inter-running of conventional services on HSR lines and vice versa occurs but is not widespread.

NOTES

1. France: US$0.24–0.31/km; Germany: US$0.34/km; Japan: US$0.29–0.31/km; Taiwan, China: US$0.13/km, using information from official travel websites, annual reports, and exchange rates. On a purchasing power parity basis, Chinese rates are about half those in other economies, except for Taiwan, China.
2. As a result, there are often vacant seats during off-peak periods, whereas tickets are difficult to obtain at peak periods, such as weekends and national holidays.
3. Although EMU trains used to run at 200 kph on the traditional railway, they now no longer run this fast where the line is shared with freight or conventional passenger services. This change improves transportation efficiency as well as passenger safety and comfort. Heavy axle load freight services affect track quality, the speed differential reduces capacity, and it is hard to simultaneously maintain track geometry suitable for both types of train at such speeds.

REFERENCE

Scales, John, Gerald Ollivier, and Paul Amos. 2011. "Railway Price Regulation in China: Time for a Rethink?" China Transport Topics No. 01, World Bank, Washington, DC. http://documents .worldbank.org/curated/en/103931468010857398/Railway-price-regulation-in-China -time-for-a-rethink.

3 Markets

The high-speed rail (HSR) service in China has been remarkably effective at attracting traffic. This chapter analyzes the markets in which the service is competitive in terms of distance, passenger characteristics, and affordability.

TRAFFIC GROWTH AND DENSITY

Since the opening of the first HSR line in 2008, total rail passenger volume has grown at 8.5 percent per year,[1] with a significant change in traffic composition (figure 3.1). Conventional rail traffic has grown at an annual rate of 0.5 percent, compared to 81.0 percent for HSR traffic (albeit from a very low base). At 1.7 billion passengers and 600 billion passenger-kilometers (pkm), China now produces

HSR and conventional service demand, 2007–17

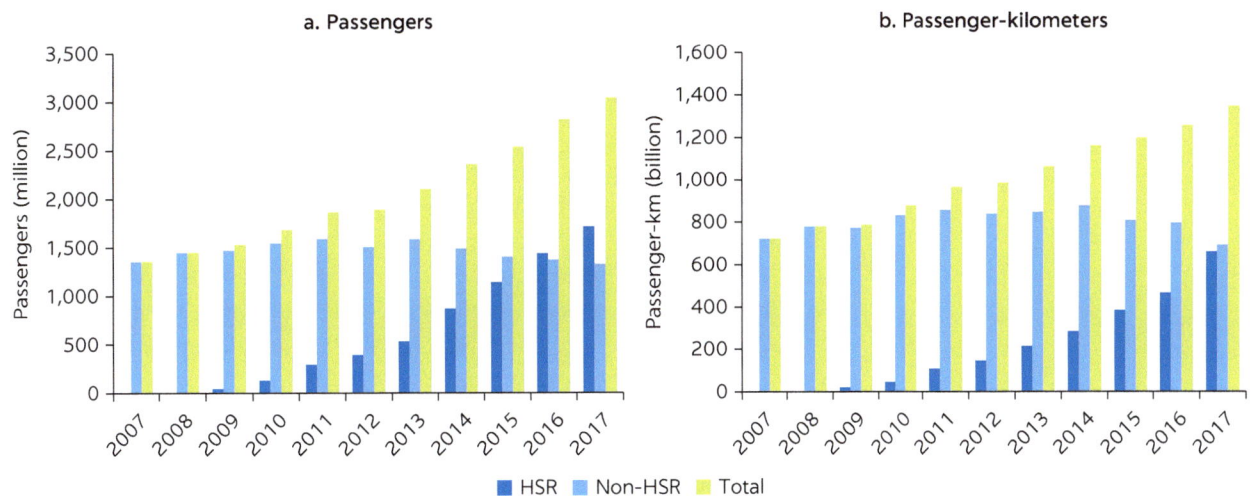

Source: Based on data from China Railway Corporation.
Note: HSR = high-speed rail.

FIGURE 3.2
High-speed rail network traffic density

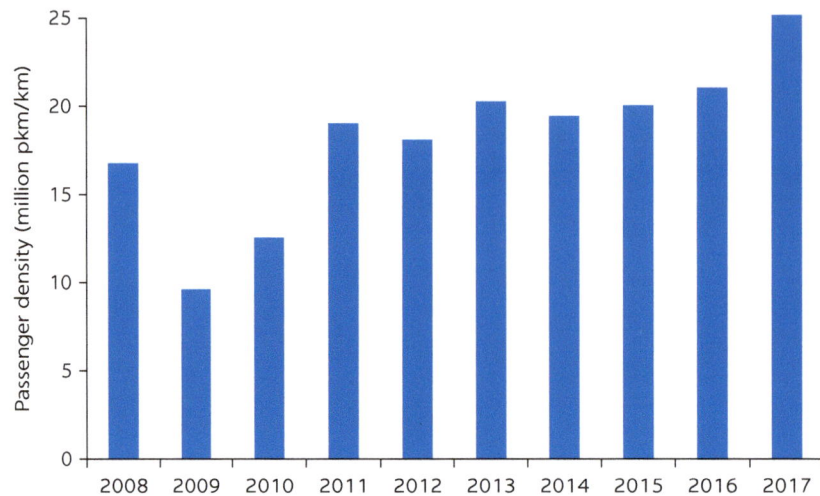

Source: Based on data from China Railway Yearbooks, 2008–17.
Note: km = kilometers; pkm = passenger-km.

more than four times as many pkm per year as the European or Japanese HSR networks (UIC 2019). Contrary to original expectations, HSR services have not yet led to a reduction in overall conventional train traffic. Rather they have created an accelerated growth in total rail traffic, which the previous network, close to full capacity, was unable to achieve. By 2017, HSR was carrying about 50 percent of all rail trips, on about 20 percent of the national rail network. Because the construction of new high-speed lines is ongoing and the HSR passenger volumes and pkm continue to grow at over 20 percent per year, these trends are likely to continue in the near future.

The average traffic density[2] on HSR main lines such as the Beijing–Shanghai line and the Beijing–Guangzhou line, and on regional intercity lines in the Yangtze and Pearl networks, is over 50 million passengers annually; however, on many of the smaller secondary lines it is 10 million or less. The average density overall on the HSR network has increased from 10 million in its first full year (2009) to the current 23 million passengers (figure 3.2). This is about twice the density of HSR in Europe and a substantial figure for a large system in its early years of existence, but it is still only two-thirds of the Japanese Shinkansen system-wide density (UIC 2019).

Although many services operate over long distances of up to 2,500 km, comparatively few passengers travel from end to end. The average trip distance in both the Beijing–Shanghai and Beijing–Guangzhou corridors in 2013 was about 500 km, and the lines also carry significant volumes of interlining traffic to and from feeder lines (about 30 percent in the case of the Beijing–Shanghai line).

When a line has opened, the typical pattern has been for demand to ramp up in the first two or three years, with traffic in the first full year of operation being about 70 percent of the steady state.

HSR PASSENGER MARKETS

Over the past five years, the World Bank and the China Railway Corporation (CRC) have conducted onboard surveys designed to obtain information on

FIGURE 3.3

Source of China Rail Highspeed passengers and passenger-kilometers, 2015

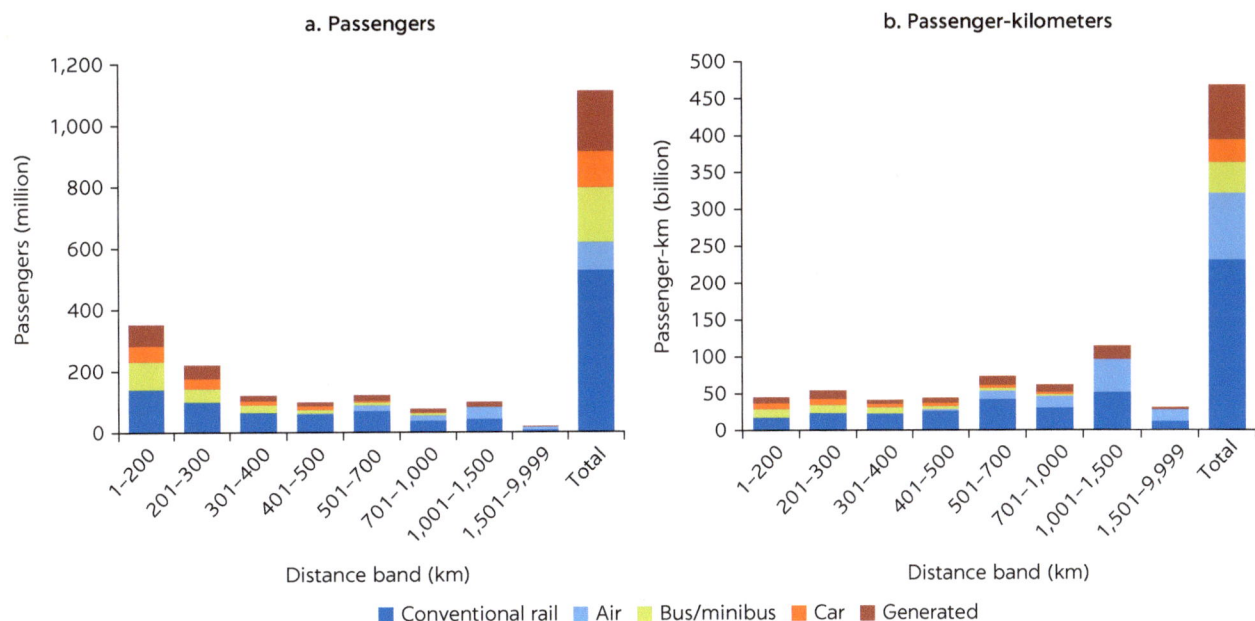

Source: World Bank–China Railway Corporation onboard surveys.

passenger characteristics, including how passengers would have traveled in the absence of HSR (figure 3.3). The characteristics naturally vary by route, but the surveys covered five major routes (two main lines, two regional lines, and one intercity line), together representing over 25 percent of the total China Rail Highspeed (CRH) demand.

In 2015, about 50 percent of both CRH passengers and pkm came from conventional rail. About 25 percent of passengers transferred from bus and car, but these riders represented only 15 percent of pkm, because they were concentrated in the shorter-distance trips. Conversely, about 10 percent of passengers transferred from air, but these riders represented about 20 percent of pkm because they were all on longer-distance trips.

Competition with air

Although air is not the major source of passengers, HSR has had a major impact on many air routes. Some short-distance air services have been completely withdrawn after an HSR line has opened; others have discounted fares or have reduced services to one or two flights each day.

Figure 3.4 shows the impact on the routes between Guangzhou and Changsha (about 600 km) and between Guangzhou and Wuhan (900 km). Flight services fell by one-half to Wuhan and two-thirds to Changsha once the HSR opened.[3]

A similar pattern can be seen in air trips between Beijing and major cities along the Guangzhou corridor. Figure 3.5 shows that the HSR had no discernable impact on the air route between Beijing and Guangzhou (a 2,000 km trip), with air passenger volume continuing to grow rapidly in this market. Demand for Beijing–Changsha flights (1,400 km) continued to grow but at a slower rate. Air traffic volume between Beijing and Wuhan (1,100 km) reduced slightly, but the reduction between Beijing and Zhengzhou (about 700 km) was so great that the air service was very substantially reduced.

FIGURE 3.4

Effect of high-speed rail on air services

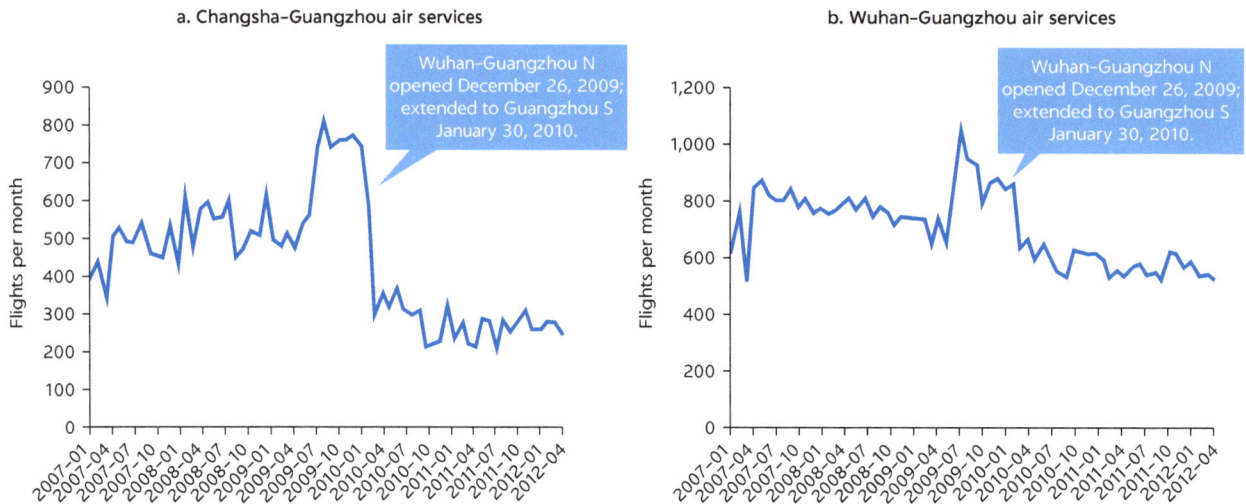

a. Changsha–Guangzhou air services

b. Wuhan–Guangzhou air services

Source: World Bank analysis of airline service offerings.

FIGURE 3.5

Effect of Beijing–Guangzhou high-speed rail on air travel

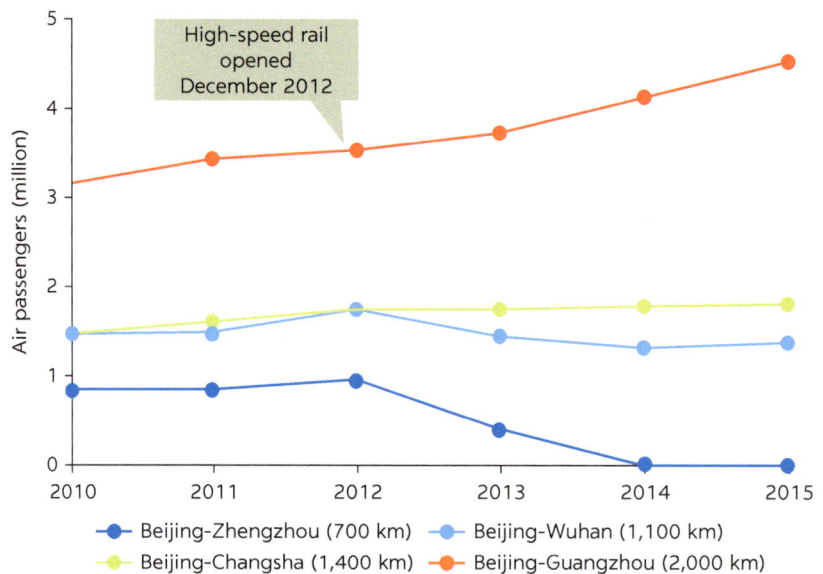

Source: World Bank analysis based on data in Statistical View of Civil Aviation.

The impact in China is thus significant up to 1,000 km (three to four hours), rather farther than is customarily expected in Europe. Besides higher speeds, this effect is also related to HSR's very high reliability combined with the fact that airports are often located far from the center of the city. For example, between Beijing and Nanjing (1,000 km) the HSR travel time is 3.5 hours, compared to 2.0 hours for air; however, the Nanjing airport is 47 km from the city center, whereas the HSR station is only 16 km from downtown. After factoring in this longer access distance, together with airport processing and air traffic control delays, passengers find the HSR service is very competitive; it now has a 60 percent market share on this route.[4] The reliability, frequency, and comfort of CRH services create strong competition for most middle-distance trips.[5]

FIGURE 3.6

Competitiveness of high-speed rail

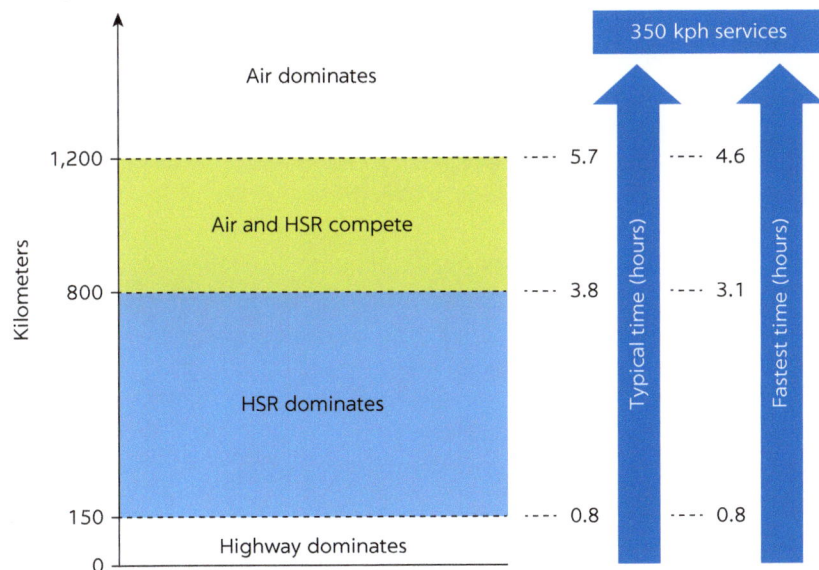

Note: The competitive ranges of the three modes are indicative. The air and high-speed rail (HSR) competitiveness was studied with a sample of 300–350-kilometer-per-hour (kph) lines. With different price and speed assumption of 200–250 kph lines, the dominance range will be slightly different.

The main competitors for shorter intercity routes are bus and private vehicles (car and minibus). These services have often been hit hard by new HSR routes, especially because rail fares on 250 kilometers per hour (kph) services are generally very competitive with, if not cheaper than, bus fares. The competing bus service between Changchun and Jilin (for which both HSR stations are in the center of the city) charged roughly the same fare as the HSR but offered a much lower quality of service. It was all but eliminated after the HSR service opened, reducing bus service from one every 5–10 minutes to one or two buses a day, traveling via intermediate towns. In other corridors (under, say, 150 km), car and bus often remain competitive, especially if the HSR station is a long distance from the city center.

Car and bus dominate the market at distances under 150 km, except for a few high-frequency regional intercity trains and where the stations are centrally located. Between 150 km and 800 km (up to four hours travel time in China), HSR dominates. The 350 kph HSR services remain competitive up to about 1,200 km (six hours travel time in China), after which air service dominates.

In summary, HSR services in China are most competitive with other modes for middle-distance journeys (figure 3.6).

NEW TRAFFIC

The onboard surveys consistently found passengers who reported they would not have traveled if HSR were not available. This share varied from corridor to corridor, but overall is estimated at 18 percent of passengers. These findings can be partially cross-checked against observed data,[6] which indicate generated traffic of 20–25 percent for the Wuhan–Guangzhou corridor, 40 percent or more for Beijing–Tianjin, and 18 percent for Changchun–Jilin.

Some of the generated trips come from new passengers who previously did not travel at all or who traveled to some other destination. These trips tend to be in the leisure and tourism markets. The Guangzhou–Guiyang line, for example, has attracted many tourists to both Guilin and Guiyang. Another documented example is the Confucian center of Qufu (see box 7.3 in chapter 7).

The onboard survey also asked if passengers had increased their travel frequency with the HSR service, comparing travel frequencies on the route in 2014 with the planned trip frequency in 2015. Over three-quarters (76 percent) of passengers reported an increase in trips for 2015, with an overall increase of 40–50 percent. Although such statements of future intent are often unreliable, the responses indicate that the increases in overall trip-making that have accompanied many HSR services are due to a combination of existing travelers making trips more frequently and completely new travelers.

IMPACT ON CONVENTIONAL RAIL SERVICES

At the initial planning stage, services on the high-speed lines were expected to handle 90 percent of corridor demand, with the remaining 10 percent using local services on the existing line. In practice, CRC found it was politically impossible to withdraw the existing services and these have continued to operate. In some of the main corridors, such as the north–south line between Beijing and Guangzhou, conventional lines still carry from one-half to two-thirds of the total passenger traffic.

Figure 3.7 shows the traffic density on sections of line in the middle of three major corridors—the Beijing–Shanghai line, the Shizheng section of the Beijing–Guangzhou line, and the Wuhan–Guangzhou line—between 2001 and 2013, before and after CRH services had started. It includes only traffic that was wholly within the corridor.

By 2013 the CRH services represented a substantial share of the market (about 45 percent) for the first two lines. The Wuhan–Guangzhou line was the first major long-distance HSR line opened, at the end of 2009. It immediately captured a large share of the market although, in this case, the introduction of the CRH services was accompanied by a significant reduction in the conventional services

FIGURE 3.7

Traffic density and market share on major corridors, 2001–13

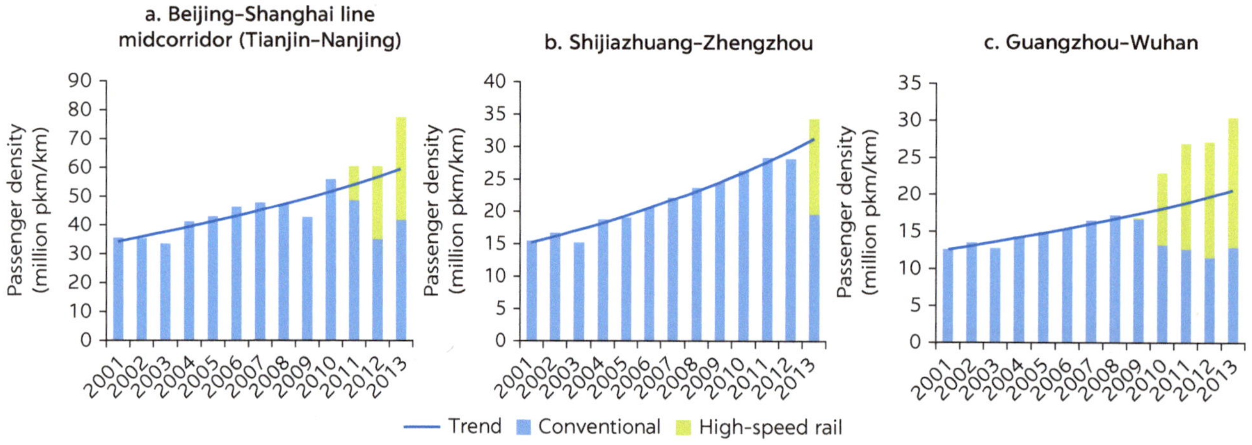

Source: World Bank analysis based on China Railway traffic data.
Note: km = kilometer; pkm = passenger-km.

so demand for these services was constrained by lack of capacity. In this corridor, the CRH services carried 58 percent of the passengers in 2013.

Demand on the existing services has remained fairly constant. Prior to the introduction of the HSR services, the conventional services were capacity-constrained: tickets were difficult to obtain, and trains were always full. It now appears the suppressed demand was significant enough to fill up the capacity freed by those transferring to HSR.

In practice the number of passenger services on the conventional railway has remained relatively constant or even increased in recent years (figure 3.8). The only exception is the Wuhan-Guangzhou corridor, the first long-distance one to operate and the one with the greatest number of complaints about services being withdrawn.

The impact of high-speed trains on conventional rail services has not been uniform across all types of trips. Table 3.1 shows the estimated share of the rail market captured by CRH services for the major pairs of cities along the Beijing–Guangzhou line. The general pattern is clear. For shorter distances between large cities (for example, Beijing–Shijiazhuang and Guangzhou–Changsha), for which the absolute fare differential between HSR and non-HSR is relatively small, HSR captures about 70–80 percent of the rail market, helped by its much

FIGURE 3.8

Train services in high-speed rail corridors, 2011–16

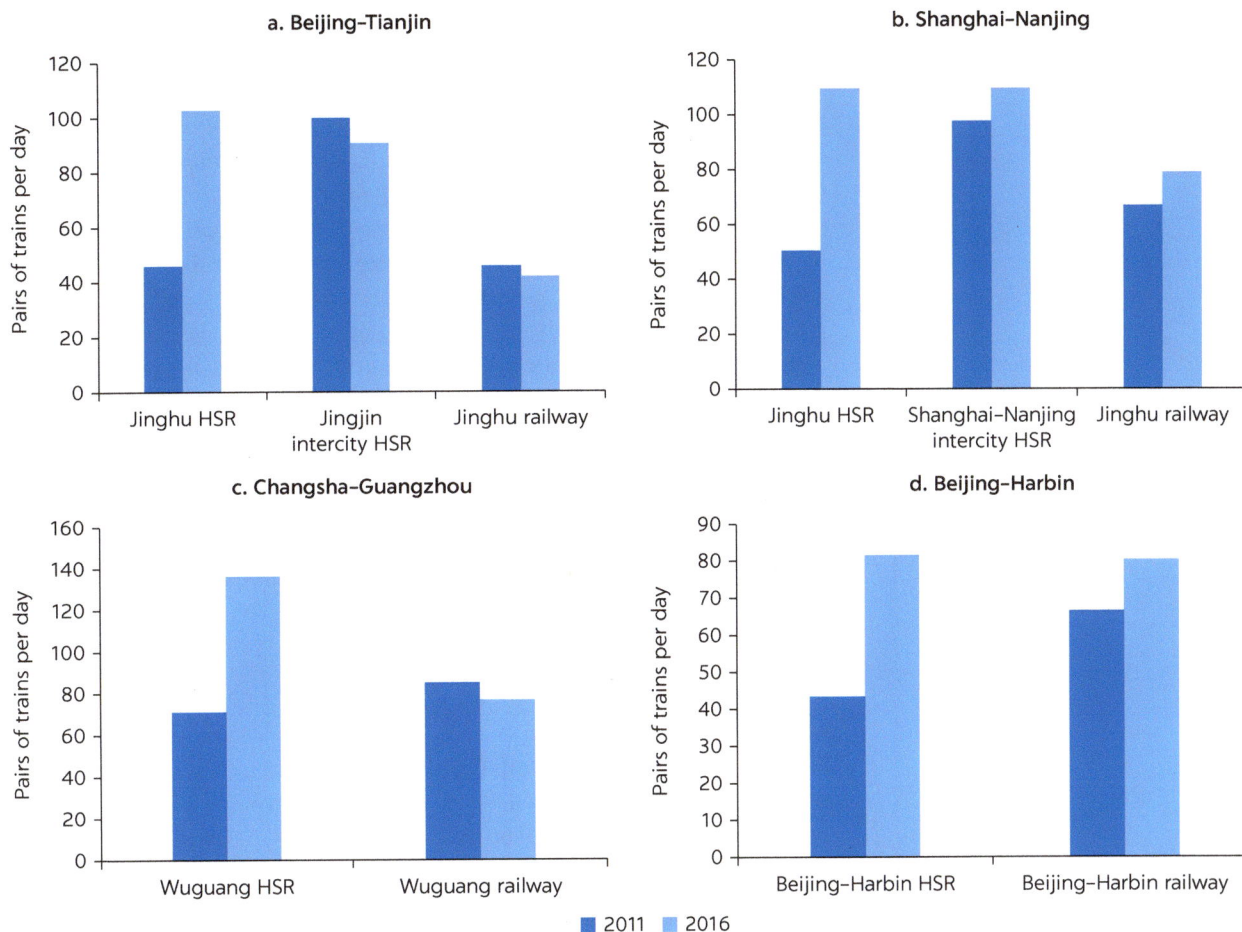

Note: HSR = high-speed rail.

TABLE 3.1 **High-speed rail share of rail market in Beijing–Guangzhou line corridor, 2013**

DISTANCE FROM BEIJING (km)	BEIJING 0	SHIJIAZHUANG 281	ZHENGZHOU 693	WUHAN 1,229	CHANGSHA 1,591	GUANGZHOU 2,298
Beijing		73	58	51	35	40
Shijiazhuang	77		51	49	42	20
Zhengzhou	55	47		46	45	24
Wuhan	52	47	44		64	64
Changsha	37	46	42	67		70
Guangzhou	37	23	24	64	71	

Source: World Bank analysis based on China Railway traffic data.

more user-friendly service frequency, schedule, and ease of buying tickets. This share then steadily reduces until, for long distances where the price differential is substantial in absolute terms, the HSR share is about 40 percent.

What are the main factors constraining what has been only a partial transfer to HSR/CRH? First, there is the issue of fare. Passengers who are time-sensitive and traveling long distances are not catching HSR but are instead flying. In the Beijing–Guangzhou line, the ratio of the fare paid for conventional trains to that paid for CRH trains is between 1:3 and 1:4, and, although this differential is relatively small in absolute terms for trips of 300 km or so (for example, Y 60–80 [US$9–12] in the case of Beijing–Shijiazhuang), it becomes a large amount (for example, Y 400–600 [US$60–90]) for a trip such as Beijing–Guangzhou.

The conventional services also partly serve different geographic markets. In many corridors, the conventional line and the HSR line are some distance apart and the conventional line has many more intermediate stations,[7] often far more conveniently located than the typical out-of-town HSR station at intermediate centers. One result is that HSR has a much smaller share of shorter-distance traffic to and from intermediate centers; it typically attracts 10–30 percent of the market.

Finally, many Chinese conventional railway services, after six speed increases, can also compete on speed, particularly because an overnight rail journey allows passengers to save on overnight accommodation. Although some electric multiple unit (EMU) sleeper services are operated on HSR lines, they are constrained by a four-hour maintenance window and cannot take full advantage of their speed.

Over time, as incomes and the value of time increase, more passengers can be expected to transfer from conventional rail services to HSR. Nonetheless, the demand for conventional services appears strong for many years to come. How this finding would translate to other countries will depend on a range of factors: the extent to which demand is supply-constrained, the fare difference between the two types of service, and geography.

AFFORDABILITY OF HSR IN CHINA

HSR attracts passengers for both business and leisure trips. Precise proportions naturally depend on the characteristics of individual routes, but surveys show business trips are typically 40–60 percent of total trips. As would be expected, a larger share of HSR passengers are traveling on business compared to conventional services, but this difference is not overwhelming.

The average of the self-reported monthly personal income[8] in the 2014–16 HSR onboard surveys ranged from Y 4,300 (US$640) for Changchun–Jilin to Y 6,700 (US$1,000) for Tianjin–Jilin, with an average of Y 5,700 (US$850).

FIGURE 3.9

Income distribution and monthly income of rail passengers, 2015

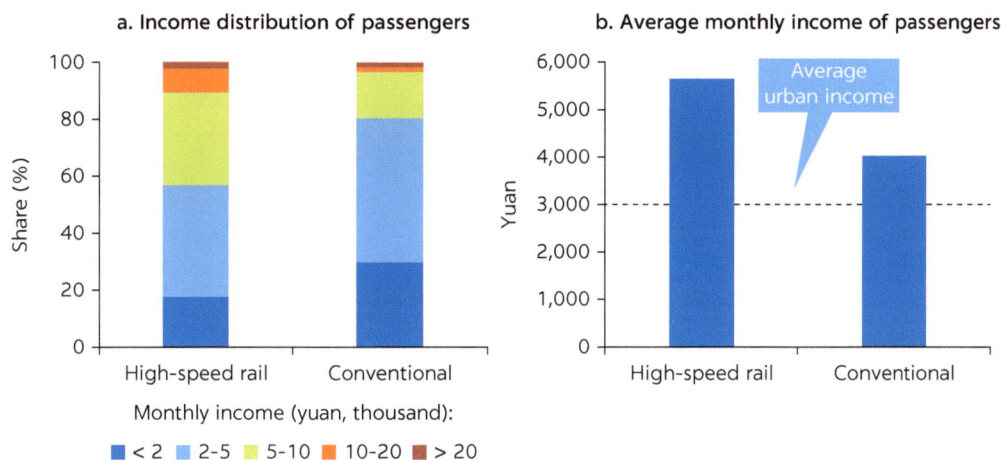

a. Income distribution of passengers

b. Average monthly income of passengers

Monthly income (yuan, thousand):

■ < 2 ■ 2-5 ■ 5-10 ■ 10-20 ■ > 20

Source: World Bank–China Railway Corporation onboard surveys.

Income on parallel conventional trains was about 65–75 percent of that on the HSR services. Figure 3.9 shows that most passengers on both types of service had monthly incomes of under Y 5,000 (US$750). At that time, the average per capita monthly income was about Y 3,000 (US$450) in eastern China.[9]

Although self-reported income figures need to be treated with caution, the survey results indicate that the HSR services are used by a broad range of income levels. A significant share of the passengers come from the lower-middle-income bracket, with nearly 60 percent of HSR users with a self-reported income of less than Y 5,000 (US$750) per month. Nonetheless, both the conventional and HSR services are used by people of all income levels (photo 3.1).

PHOTO 3.1

Family traveling on Guiyang–Guangzhou high-speed rail

Source: © Mengke Chen/World Bank. Permission required for reuse.

In many ways, the HSR seems to have filled a gap in the type of services previously offered, and demonstrated that customers are willing to pay more for a higher-quality service.

Highlights

- HSR services have drawn about half their passengers from conventional rail services. About 25 percent come from bus and car and about 10 percent from air. Some 15–20 percent are new passengers (generated traffic).
- HSR is very competitive with other modes for trip distances between 150 and 800 km. Because of its high speed and service frequency in China, HSR remains competitive up to 1,200 km.

- Conventional services are still heavily used—they are much cheaper than HSR (by 3:1 or 4:1) and provide services to stations not served by HSR. Shifting passengers has freed capacity on conventional services, which can now serve pent-up demand.
- HSR fares in China are low compared to those in other countries, enabling HSR to attract passengers from all income levels.

NOTES

1. Passenger-kilometers grew rather more slowly, at about 6.5 percent per year, because the average trip length on many HSR corridors is much shorter than for conventional services.
2. Defined as the HSR pkm divided by the average length of HSR lines in operation for the year.
3. By 2017 flights to and from Wuhan had recovered slightly to about 600 per month, but Changsha remains at about 200.
4. Although many HSR stations are also located outside the city center, providing high-quality transport links from these stations to downtown areas can enhance HSR attractiveness.
5. In response to this competition, 2016 domestic airfares were reformed in 2016 as noted earlier. Airlines are now allowed to set their own fares when the route distance is shorter than 800 km or when it is longer than 800 km but competing with an HSR service.
6. Air and rail data are available; bus passengers can be estimated from service frequencies; data are not available for automobile travel.
7. Station spacing on the HSR lines is typically 50 km, compared to 8–10 km on the conventional network.
8. In the Chinese context this income is generally understood as the monthly average take-home pay or regular receipts from pension and properties.
9. But ranging from Y 4,000 in Beijing and Shanghai to just over Y 2,000 in Jilin.

REFERENCE

UIC (International Railway Union). 2019. "High Speed Traffic in the World." Fact sheet, UIC, Paris. https://uic.org/IMG/pdf/20190122_high_speed_passenger_km.pdf.

4 Construction

This chapter examines how China has managed to build such a large high-speed rail (HSR) network in such a short time and with a remarkable record of on-time, on-budget completion of investment projects. China has a highly integrated supply chain for both construction and rolling stock, which reduces project capital cost. Standardization of designs and management methods has also been an important influence, as have strong contract management and supervision.

DESIGN STANDARDS AND CONSTRUCTION COST

The technical specifications used for HSR lines are standardized (see table 4.1).

Figure 4.1 shows the construction cost of 60 projects. The average cost of a double-track HSR line (including signaling, electrification, and facilities) is about Y 139 million/km (US$20.6 million/km)[1] for a 350 kph HSR line, about Y 114 million (US$16.9 million) for a 250 kph HSR line, and about Y 104 million (US$15.4 million) for a 200 kph HSR line.[2] These costs are at least 40 percent cheaper than construction costs in Europe (European Court of Auditors 2018, 35).[3] The large construction program over the past decade has been a factor in these low costs, with specialist teams and mobile production facilities (for example, for bridge beams) moving directly from project to project. Contractors are able to amortize the investment in specialized equipment (see photos 4.1 and 4.2) and production facilities over multiple projects.

As shown in figure 4.1, however, the cost of individual projects of the same speed can vary by up to 100 percent, depending on engineering conditions, project scope, and land acquisition and demolition costs. The cost of a 350 kph alignment compared to a 250 kph alignment for any given project is 10 percent to 30 percent greater, on the basis of estimates from feasibility studies, which typically include comparisons of different speed alternatives.

TABLE 4.1 **HSR technical standards by maximum speed**

			350 kph	300 kph[a]	250 kph	200 kph
Alignment	Distance between centers of tracks of main line (m)		5.0	4.8	4.6	4.2
	Minimum horizontal radius (m)	Ballastless	Normal 7,000 Difficult 5,500	Normal 5,000 Difficult 4,000	Normal 3,200 Difficult 2,800	Normal 2,200 Difficult 2,000
		Ballasted	Normal 7,000 Difficult 6,000	Normal 5,000 Difficult 4,500	Normal 3,500 Difficult 3,000	
	Minimum vertical (m)		25,000	25,000	20,000	Normal 15,000 Difficult 10,000
Track	Type of track		Ballastless		Ballasted or ballastless	Mostly ballasted, sometimes ballastless
Subgrade	Subgrade width (m)	Ballastless	13.6	13.4	13.2	11.5 or 11.7 (without cable trough on the subgrade shoulder) 13 (with cable trough on the subgrade shoulder)
		Ballasted	n.a.		13.4	10.3 (without cable trough on the subgrade shoulder) 11.8 (with cable trough on the subgrade shoulder)
	Subgrade thickness (m)	Ballastless	2.7	2.7	2.7	2.7
		Ballasted	n.a.		3	3
	Postconstruction subgrade settlement (cm)	Ballastless	≤1.5	≤1.5	≤1.5	≤1.5
		Ballasted	n.a.		General sections ≤10. Transition sections at bridge abutments ≤5	General sections ≤15. Transition sections at bridge abutments ≤8
Bridge and culverts	Uniform settlement of abutment or pier (mm)	Ballastless	≤20	≤20	≤20	≤20
		Ballasted	n.a.		≤30	≤50
	Differential settlement of adjacent abutments and piers (mm)	Ballastless	≤5	≤5	≤5	≤10
		Ballasted	n.a.		≤15	≤20
Tunnel	Effective area (m²)		Double-track tunnels ≥100		Double-track tunnels ≥90	Double-track tunnels ≥72
			Single-track tunnels ≥70		Single-track tunnels ≥58	Single-track tunnels ≥35
Signaling	Train operation control		CTCS-3		CTCS-3 or CTCS-2	CTCS-2
Communications	GSM-R system		Single network interlaced coverage		CTCS-3: Single network interlaced coverage. CTCS-2: common single network interlaced coverage	Single network interlaced coverage

continued

TABLE 4.1, *continued*

		350 kph	300 kphᵃ	250 kph	200 kph
Power supply	Traction power supply	AT power supply mode			Direct power supply with current return wire
Overhead contact line system	Subgrade mast	H-beam mast generally used for single-mast of subgrade		Concrete round mast generally used for single-mast of subgrade	Concrete round mast generally used for single-mast of subgrade
	Support device	Aluminum alloy wrist arm generally used		Steel wrist arm generally used	Steel wrist arm generally used
Electric power	High-pressure cabinet of distribution stations	Gas cabinet		Air cabinet	Air cabinet

Note: The design of 250, 300, and 350 kilometer per hour (kph) lines follow the Code for Design for High Speed Railway (TB10621-2014); and the design of 200 kph lines follows the Code for Design of Intercity Railway Line (TB10623-2014). AT = autotransformer; CTCS = Chinese Train Control System; GSM-R = Global System for Mobile Communications-Railway; n.a. = not applicable.
a. In practice, no 300 kph line has yet been built in China.

FIGURE 4.1

Construction cost of high-speed rail projects in China

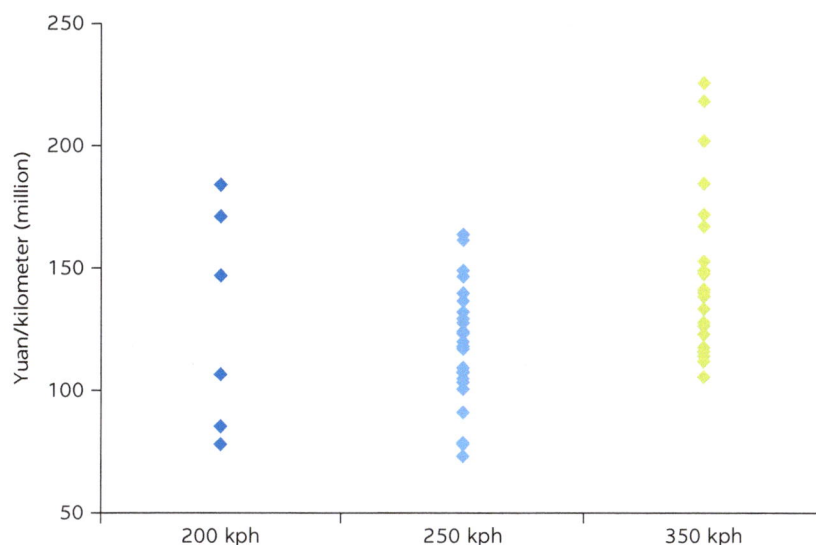

Source: World Bank Analysis based on data from China Railway Corporation.
Note: kph = kilometers per hour.

THE HSR SUPPLY CHAIN

The HSR supply chain has four main branches: engineering construction, equipment manufacturing, technology research, and operation management. The size of the HSR network development in China has provided a large enough market for each of these branches to be fully developed.

The construction and management of an HSR line is the responsibility of the relevant joint venture (JV) company. The JV normally contracts to one or more of the eight Chinese railway survey and design corporations for survey and design services. Construction and construction supervision are contracted to one or more of many construction and supervision enterprises, most of which belong to

Setting precast bridge beams on Zhanghu railway line

Source: © Martha Lawrence/World Bank. Permission required for reuse.

China Railway Construction Corporation Ltd. (CRCC) and China Railway Group Ltd. (CREC), some of the world's largest construction contractors.

China also has a complete chain of railway equipment manufacturing. The equipment manufacturing enterprises are licensed by the National Railway Administration (NRA), which is also responsible for the supervision and inspection of product quality. Currently the main electric multiple unit (EMU) plants are in Qingdao, Tangshan, Changchun, Jiangmen, and Nanjing. They belong to China Railway Rolling Stock Corporation (CRRC), which produces 31 versions of EMU products. China's high-speed trains cost only one-third to one-half as much as their overseas counterparts.

The four main categories of rail infrastructure equipment manufacturing—turnouts and switches, signal control software and equipment, communication

Specialized equipment for transporting bridge beams

Source: © Nanyan Zhou/World Bank. Permission required for reuse.

equipment, and traction power supply—are supplied by more than 130 enterprises in total.

The technology and research development for China Railways consists of three groups: enterprises, scientific research institutes, and colleges and universities. Most enterprises integrate research and development with manufacturing, and the industry–university Research Cooperation Mechanism promotes development. Many of the major railway research institutes, such as the China Academy of Railway Sciences and the China Railway Economic and Planning Research Institute, are subsidiaries of China Railway Corporation (CRC).

An important factor has been that the major contractors and suppliers, being assured of a continuing program of projects, have invested in equipment and facilities that have enabled them in turn to increase efficiency and reduce costs.

This level of self-sufficiency and the associated industrial supply chains brought significant scale advantages that are unlikely to be available elsewhere. The extent to which other countries can copy the practice of China depends on their individual situations. Nevertheless, many features of the Chinese system do offer useful lessons to other countries considering HSR projects.

PROJECT PLANNING, DESIGN, AND APPROVAL

Each year, the CRC Planning Department prepares a plan for the work to be done in the following year. This plan is reviewed internally and then approved.

Prior to 2015, prefeasibility studies were undertaken for each project. Since 2015 the process has been simplified and now begins with the feasibility study proper, which is submitted to the National Development and Reform Commission for examination and approval.[4] Design works are normally divided into two stages, preliminary design and construction design.

For the preliminary design, the CRC Planning Department makes the work plan. The corporation hires an engineering design consultant (that is, a design corporation) to complete the preliminary design according to the plan, which is submitted to CRC. The appraisal center within CRC reviews the preliminary design and gives comments, and then the preliminary design is sent to different departments in CRC for approval. For JV projects (this includes all HSR projects) the preliminary design also needs to be approved by the relevant partner (such as, the provincial government). The preliminary design strictly follows the scope of construction, standards, and investment as in the feasibility study; any substantial modifications must be approved by the deputy general manager of CRC.

The draft design, which should closely follow the preliminary design, is then undertaken by the engineering design corporation. The draft is reviewed by the Project Management Center of CRC, which has the capacity to review complex engineering components like bridges, tunnels, and major stations. Once approved, the draft design can be modified only by specific authorization through design change provisions.

Before 2015, the construction start-up plan also needed to be approved before starting construction. This requirement has now been removed; instead the JV is required to closely follow the relevant regulations, including the following:

- The project conforms to the relevant plans and policies.
- A competent person or authority has signed the design documents and delivery agreement with the design institute.
- A safety assessment management system has been established.
- The preliminary design of the project, total budget estimates, and construction estimates have been approved and the construction drawings reviewed.
- The tendering process of general contractors and construction supervisors has been completed.
- The project capital fund and other construction funds have been secured in line with state regulations. The loan contract has been signed in line with the feasibility approval, and the source bank has also been approved.

Competitive tendering is used for all HSR investments including for project design, construction services, and rolling stock. A tendering and bidding center in each province handles all engineering and service tendering. Because CRC is the largest shareholder for most JVs, most HSR tenders are handled by the Beijing tendering and bidding center. Bids are reviewed by an expert committee, and the top three bidders are selected. The tendering company may then choose among these bidders.

Once completed, the JV reports to CRC (primarily the Construction Management Department and Project Management Center) and to the NRA for some aspects.

The timeline of China's HSR planning, design, and approval is rather fast. Usually, it takes less than a year from the start of feasibility study proper to the start of construction.

CONSTRUCTION OVERSIGHT AND SUPERVISION

Both CRC and local government oversee HSR construction, while the JV's supervision consultant provides day-to-day project supervision.

CRC's main agencies for oversight are the following:

- The **Construction Management Department** prepares the railway construction standards and standard costs, oversees the construction management system, and supervises the implementation of standard designs. It undertakes the centralized management of bidding, contract performance, project quality, and production safety. At the project level, it provides centralized management of the construction work, guides the completion acceptance of projects, and guides coordination on major issues. At the industry level, it oversees the railway construction sector and provides guidance and assessments to individual construction units and monitors corporate and individual staff qualifications.
- The **Safety Supervision and Administration Bureau** prepares the safety regulations and systems and supervises their implementation at both the macro and micro levels. It draws up and supervises the implementation of the safety assessment plan for new railway lines before opening.
- The **Project Management Center** is responsible for the organization and day-to-day supervision of large and medium-sized railway construction projects. This covers construction plans, construction quality and safety, acceptance, and commissioning.
- The **Engineering Quality Supervision Bureau** supervises and inspects engineering quality and construction safety, including any investigation of accidents during construction.

The local government's main agencies for oversight are the following:

- The **Safety Supervision Bureau** undertakes detailed supervision of the project, inspecting construction at regular intervals, investigating accidents, and inspecting the project prior to opening.
- The **Quality Supervision Department** similarly undertakes detailed supervision and examination of construction quality.

The JV hires a Construction Supervisor, responsible for the supervision of day-to-day operation and for the performance of construction contractors, in terms of both physical output and project management.

CONSTRUCTION MANAGEMENT

In 2007, the Ministry of Railways (MOR) introduced standardized management of construction projects. The key principle of this management model, which is applied to all HSRs, is that "everything has a standard, everything has a process, everything has a responsible person." By introducing standard procedures, this approach has saved construction costs and time and has avoided rework and wasted resources. It has also promoted continuous improvement of construction standards and helped improve the level of safety.

The model has four key features.

- It is *normative*: From the top-level design to the basic implementation, there are specified standards and norms. At the construction site, procurement, personnel allocation, site layout, and production safety are all covered by regulations, thereby establishing a standardized site and a standardized team.
- It is *systematic*: A comprehensive collaborative relationship must be established between the various subsystems to guarantee performance and ensure that the whole is greater than the sum of the parts.
- It is *versatile*: The framework can be applied across all regions, natural environments, and contractors.
- It is *flexible*: Within this overall framework, individual contractors can nevertheless formulate their own rules and regulations for their subprojects. CRC (and previously MOR) prepared the Measures for the Administration of Railway Contracts, which provide the framework within which an individual JV can create project contract management structures reflecting the specific characteristics of each project.

China has a comprehensive set of environmental management laws and regulations for construction projects, including environmental management regulations and norms specifically for railway projects. CRC pays very high attention to the enforcement of the environmental management system in a railway construction project. It established a "Six in One" policy for railway projects in 2007, which requires integration of six targets in any project—that is, quality, safety, environment, construction period, investment, and technical innovation. The system follows a mitigation hierarchy approach that is in line with international good practice—that is, significant effort in avoidance of environmental risks/impacts upfront, followed by minimization of impacts through sound project design, comprehensive mitigation measures, and offset measures when necessary. For example, to manage noise impact, measures are taken to minimize noise through technical design (such as seamless tracks), erection of sound barriers, and resettling people away from the track where necessary.

Procedurally, an Environmental Impact Assessment (EIA) and Environmental Management Plan (EMP) must be prepared and approved by the Ministry of Environmental Protection. Upon project completion, an environmental acceptance examination is conducted by a third-party consultant engaged by the project owner to verify the implementation and compliance of environmental measures as per EIA/EMP requirements. Environmental acceptance is part of the approval for trial operation, formal operation, and final project completion after one year of operation.

Similarly, China has a comprehensive land administration law and implementing regulations that govern land acquisition and provide for compensation to people affected by projects. All railway projects are carried out in accordance with the national law and regulations.

Under the standard management model, each party takes a different role in the project construction. Figure 4.2 shows the managerial structure of HSR construction:

CRC oversees the JV and is responsible for preparing the construction management standards, reviewing and approving the design, monitoring

FIGURE 4.2

Construction management structure

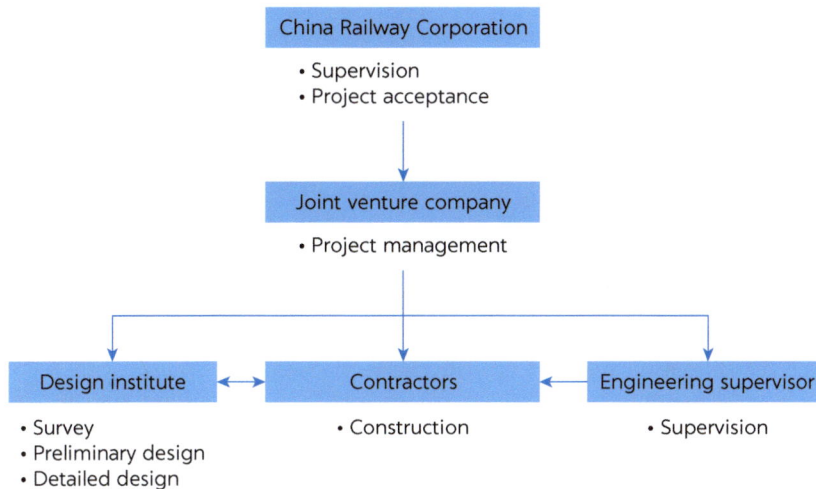

the implementation of construction standards, and assessing and accepting the project upon completion.

The **JV** hires the design institutes, contractors, and engineering supervisors to carry out the work. As the project manager, the JV is responsible for securing the capital; managing the contracts; coordinating between designers, contractors, and engineering supervisors; inspecting the construction work; controlling and giving instructions on the work progress, quality, and safety; and reporting to CRC. The JV's project managers have clear responsibilities and authority to carry them out. They typically stay for the full duration of the project, ensuring a clear chain of responsibility for the implementation of the project.

The **design institute** is the surveyor and engineering designer of the project, and is responsible for surveying, preliminary design, and detailed design. In most cases, there is only one design institute doing all the survey and design from the feasibility proper phase to the construction phase.[5]

Contractors build the project according to the detailed design made by the design institute. At the operational level, the "Jiazi Group" model to organize the workers was developed to ensure the quality of construction work. Under this model, qualified professional managers and engineers from the general contractors will form subgroups called Jiazi Groups to manage individual construction tasks. The Jiazi Group directly instructs and manages individual workers to carry out the construction work, ensure operational and technical standards are met, and ensure the work progress follows the work plan. Individual workers sign individual work contracts with the general contractor. In comparison, under the traditional subcontracting model, workers are managed by subcontractors, who may be technically less capable and responsible. Thus the Jiazi Group model better ensures the quality of construction work (see box 4.1 for further discussion of the contract management system).

An **engineering supervisor** is hired to supervise the day-to-day work of the contractors to ensure construction quality and safety; the engineering supervisor reports to the JV.

BOX 4.1

JV contract management system

The primary purpose of establishing the contract management structure is to regulate the establishment, performance, alteration, and termination of railway construction contracts; prevent and reduce contract disputes; and safeguard the legitimate rights and interests of the parties to the contract.

Contract management is subject to centralized management and graded responsibilities. The joint venture (JV) is the main body for contract management and is responsible for establishing a contract management system and appointing contract management personnel including full-time legal advisers when necessary. A contract management team shall be set up, chaired by the general manager with vice managers for each department.

The JV is responsible for negotiating and drafting the relevant technical clauses of the contract, which are also reviewed by the contract management steering group.

The contract manager of the JV conducts an annual inspection, reporting to the Construction Bureau of the Regional Administration and the Enterprise Management Law Office. The JV also organizes both regular and ad hoc inspections.

Finally, the JV establishes contract management records and regularly conducts statistical analysis. After the contract has been completed, the contractor submits a work report to the JV, and all contract documents are archived.

INCENTIVE MECHANISMS IN HSR PROJECT CONSTRUCTION

The characteristics of the construction company's production methods and engineering projects determine the details of the project manager's incentives. The responsibility and risk of HSR projects are shared at three levels.

1. The construction company is the bidding and contracting party and takes the profitability and reputation risks on each project.
2. The construction company's project manager controls the quality, cost, and timeliness of the construction, and takes the managerial risk.
3. The construction workers carry out the construction work and take operational risks.

All these three levels share the profits of HSR projects according to their responsibility and risk.

The incentive mechanism for the contractor's project manager should be designed to align the project manager's personal benefits with the long-term interests of the construction company. The assessment of project managers is based not only on how much profit has been made by the project but also on a thorough consideration of project quality, safety, construction management, contract performance, and environmental impacts, which influence the project company's long-term benefits.

The project manager's financial compensation typically consists of a basic salary and a performance-based bonus, supplemented with nonfinancial incentives and rewards. The basic salary is normally determined by the scale of the project, classified by the construction cost of the project (excluding subcontracts), with adjusting factors considering the project location and construction difficulty. This salary is supplemented by a performance-based bonus, reflecting performance and risks. Taking one rail construction company as an example, the performance-based bonus is established as a function of the basic salary, ranging from 0 up to 150 percent. Factors considered typically include construction safety, engineering quality, financial management and reporting, on-time completion, and relationships with external parties (environment, water, and so on). These factors are assessed on a quarterly basis with the average at the end of the project used to determine the final bonus. In addition, in many cases, a portion of the profits from the project is given to the project management team, which provides significant incentives for them to save costs.

Highlights

- Chinese construction costs average about Y 139 million/km (US$20.6 million/km) for 350 kph lines, about Y 114 million/km (US$16.9 million/km) for 250 kph lines, and about Y 104 million/km (US$15.4 million/km) for a 200 kph HSR line. These costs are at least 40 percent cheaper than in Europe.
- Although labor costs are lower in China, a key factor in the lower cost and rapid and efficient HSR construction has been the standardization of designs and procedures.
- The steady stream of projects has also encouraged the creation of a capable, competitive supply industry.

- The large HSR investment program, which is not changed once approved, has also encouraged the development of an innovative and competitive capacity for equipment manufacture and construction and the ability to amortize the capital cost of construction equipment over multiple projects.
- Project managers have clear responsibilities and delegated authority to carry them out. They typically stay for the full duration of the project, ensuring a clear chain of responsibility for the implementation of the project. Their compensation includes a significant component of incentive compensation related to performance.

NOTES

1. Construction costs of various years are converted to 2017 yuan using gross domestic product deflator to account for inflation; inflation in 2018 is assumed at 2 percent. The 2017 average exchange rate US$/Y = 6.75 was taken to convert yuan to U.S. dollars.
2. The average cost of 200 kph HSRs is estimated with a sample of six lines because of data availability. Because of the small sample size, these numbers should be treated with caution.
3. Based on a sample of 10 lines.
4. In some cases, the approval of railway construction projects can be done jointly by CRC and the provincial government, if the construction relates to no more than one province.
5. There are eight railway design institutes in China: (i) China Railway Design Corporation affiliated with CRC; (ii) China Railway First Survey and Design Institute Group Co.; (iii) China Railway Siyuan Survey and Design Group Co.; (iv) China Railway Fifth Survey and Design Insitute Group Co. and (v) China Railway Shanghai Design Institute Group Co. affiliated with CRCC; and (vi) China Railway Eryuan Engineering Group Co., (vii) China Railway Liuyuan Group Co., and (viii) Railway Engineering Consulting Group Co. affiliated with CREC.

REFERENCE

European Court of Auditors. 2018. "A European High-Speed Rail Network: Not a Reality but an Ineffectual Patchwork." Special Report No. 19, European Court of Auditors, Luxembourg City.

5 Testing, Commissioning, and Safety

The China Railway Corporation (CRC) has a well-developed system for the testing and commissioning of all lines and then, once they are in operation, of ensuring their safety. High-speed rail (HSR) is no different from the rest of the network in the principles that are followed. Because of its higher speeds, however, HSR does have more elaborate systems and procedures for ensuring safe operations on a day-to-day basis.

COMPLETION ACCEPTANCE OF NEW LINES

The completion acceptance of HSR is divided into five stages:

1. Static acceptance
2. Dynamic acceptance
3. Preliminary acceptance
4. Safety assessment
5. Formal acceptance.

Static acceptance is the process of ensuring the quality of project design and equipment installation. Normally, it is organized by the Regional Administration (RA). It consists of self-inspection from the construction contractors with confirmation from the joint venture (JV).

Dynamic acceptance normally follows static acceptance. The RA organizes a "joint test" of engineering quality. The joint test uses a high-speed integrated test train and related equipment to make repeated runs over the line at varying speeds under a wide range of operating conditions to ensure all systems (such as communications, signals, braking) function in a properly integrated manner.

China's HSR joint test also covers operational systems, including organization and management, progress management, safety management, and quality management. Specific regulations, covering all aspects of HSR operations are developed in conjunction with the various departments of the RA. These regulations formalize three layers of management: administration (typically by the RA), the construction project management agency (with other relevant units), and the testing organization (the inspection department).

Preliminary acceptance is normally done after completion of dynamic acceptance, organized by the acceptance committee of CRC.

Normally, the safety assessment follows the preliminary acceptance. This process inspects safety management, equipment and facilities, regulations, and staff quality to evaluate whether the line is ready to operate. Safety assessment is usually organized by the safety supervision administration of CRC. After the safety assessment is passed, the initial operation can be started.

Formal acceptance usually occurs after a year of trial operation. It is the process of checking and evaluating the overall condition of a construction project after one year from its initial operation. The HSR line is then put into formal operation. Normally, formal acceptance is organized by the National Development and Reform Commission (NDRC) or the National Railway Administration (NRA).

HSR SAFETY

Since 2013, rail safety management has been implemented by CRC under the supervision and regulation of NRA. NRA is responsible for the development of railway safety management regulations. CRC is responsible for the supervision and implementation of NRA's regulations, complemented with internal standards and regulation, undertaken by teams at individual stations, depots, and districts.

The first Railway Law, promulgated in 1990, set out the basic principles of railway safety management. In 2014, Regulations on the Administration of Railway Safety were issued, which have become the fundamental guidelines for safety management. They cover the basic policy and principles, as well as the organization and implementation of railway safety management. A series of safety regulations have been issued on specific aspects such as emergency rescue, accident investigations, and driving. These also meet the requirements of the more general law on safe industrial production. With the rapid development of China's HSRs, the law was revised in 2015, with specific reference to HSR safety management. A specific set of technical regulations for HSR have been developed, complementing the existing laws and regulations for conventional railways.

The HSR safety management system has four principal components: System Guarantee, Technical Equipment Control, Personnel Organization, and Emergency Rescue. The System Guarantee provides the legal and regulatory basis for HSR safety management, while the Technical Equipment Control provides the technical guarantee. The Personnel Organization provides a solid human resources base, and Emergency Rescue provides the emergency support programs.

China's approach to railway safety risk control focuses on safety throughout the entire life cycle, combining technical solutions in the design phase, project quality in the construction phase, and inspection and maintenance in the operation phase. It considers the three elements that affect safety—technology, personnel, and the external environment—and its objectives are a sound detection and monitoring system, effective mechanisms for training personnel, and a comprehensive operational control system.

The HSR Train Control System automatically monitors train operation and the central technical equipment, ensuring operational safety and efficiency for a range of speed levels. It includes ground equipment, vehicle equipment, a signal data transmission network, and vehicle information transmission equipment. The ground equipment provides the line parameters, distance, and route status. The onboard equipment provides the driver with information on speed and location through a cab interface. The signal data transmission network and train-to-ground information transmission equipment complete the ground equipment and vehicle equipment information exchange.

To operate safely under high speed, the HSR lines are fully segregated to avoid the invasion of foreign bodies. Viaduct bridges and tunnels are used on a large scale for HSR lines, which is a natural segregation from people and animals. For at-grade sections, the HSR tracks are fully fenced with culverts reserved for people and livestock to cross over. Also, HSR lines are monitored through video monitors. Cameras installed on mobile communication signal towers send the video to a monitoring center 24/7. Moreover, a restricted area is designated as 10–20 meters from each side of the line, where activities such as farming, mining, and waste disposal are forbidden.

Strong winds, heavy rainfall (and snow), and earthquakes can all also affect the safe operation of HSRs. Monitoring systems have been established for natural disasters and foreign bodies on the track, and they will automatically initiate countermeasures to ensure the safety of high-speed trains. Wind speed gauges, rain gauges, and snow depth meters are installed on catenary pillars and on the ground. An earthquake monitoring subsystem monitors the situation along the railway line; when the detected earthquake acceleration reaches a set alarm threshold, the system automatically alerts the train control system, which then controls the train running. Earthquake alarm information is also sent to the traction substation, stopping the power supplied to the catenary network through the traction substation, and stopping the train in an emergency; simultaneously, information is sent to the operation dispatch center for the organization of emergency rescue and quick repair of the line.

At some locations, highways cross the railways by an overbridge, creating a risk that fallen objects could enter an HSR line. These locations are also equipped with monitoring devices that alert the train control system and trains operating on the line sections affected.

Given the large number of new technologies, new equipment, and new systems associated with HSR, specialized training of HSR personnel plays an important role in ensuring rail safety. CRC has established an HSR technical training center, a railway continuing education high-tech base, and an HSR accident rescue training center to form a three-level HSR training system.

At the same time, CRC issued a series of regulations on the technical training of HSR staff, covering the training and qualifications for technical and professional staff, the training of other staff, and procedures for HSR traffic control. This training covered both theoretical study and practice across all aspects of HSR operation.

Safety management has not been confined to the operating staff but also applies to passengers. Passenger security and baggage checking have been introduced at all HSR stations. In addition, CRC conducts HSR safety education and publicity for passengers through a range of methods. On-train safety announcements are made, and safety warning signs are attached to infrastructure in populated areas.

If accidents or incidents do occur, an HSR emergency management system has been established, with links to local governments and emergency response units. This includes procedures for the emergency evacuation of passengers, derailment rescue and recovery, train fire emergencies, and equipment failures. All RAs stock emergency relief supplies and reserve capital perennially to provide a rapid response to such emergencies.

INFRASTRUCTURE MAINTENANCE

Rigorous infrastructure inspection and maintenance are part of the safety system in the operational phase. Table 5.1 shows the inspection program. China mainly uses high-speed integrated inspection trains and special inspection teams to carry out infrastructure inspections. These inspections cover both track and catenary and transmit data to the railway infrastructure inspection data center for analysis to highlight potential maintenance priorities. The first train on each HSR line each day is the "confirm train," which checks that the HSR equipment is in good condition to operate the first passenger train. Comprehensive inspection trains ("Doctor Yellow") run every 10 days to carry out a physical examination of HSR infrastructure (track, signals and communications, catenaries, and wheel–rail interaction).

In addition to the dynamic checks by the inspection trains, CRC also uses a maintenance window of 240 minutes each night to perform a static periodic inspection of the line and make any necessary track geometry adjustments. According to the type and level of HSR faults detected, the railway works department repairs or replaces the track and catenary components during the maintenance window and restores them to normal conditions.

Communication and signals maintenance focuses on preventive maintenance using a combination of ground monitoring, data from the inspection trains, and the remote monitoring of the on-train systems.

TABLE 5.1 High-speed rail track maintenance inspection program

METHOD	CONTENT	EQUIPMENT	INTERVAL
Dynamic	Track geometry status	Integrated test train	10 days
	Vehicle dynamic response	Integrated test train	10 days
	Wheel and rail dynamics	Integrated test train	10 days
	Unit status	Comprehensive inspection train	Quarter
	Rail detecting	Rail detection train	Month
	Subgrade, track bed status	Address radar detection train	Year
	Track stiffness	Track loading train	Year
	Tunnel lining status	Tunnel inspection train	Year
Static	Track geometry status	Track inspection equipment	Month
	Line profile	Profile tester	Year
	Tunnel, track bed surface condition	Laser profile measuring instrument checker	Year
	Switch and regulator	Inspection equipment	Year
	Rail status	Flaw detector, profile inspection equipment	Month
	Track	Track monitoring device	Year
	Precision measurement network	Total station precision measurement car	Year

ELECTRIC MULTIPLE UNIT MAINTENANCE

As with infrastructure, China's electric multiple unit (EMU) maintenance currently focuses on preventive repairs with other maintenance only as required. The vehicles have over 3,000 automatic sensors monitoring the status of moving parts. These sensors transmit information to the EMU depot/workshop to help guide the specific maintenance undertaken. The maintenance cycle is largely based on usage, supplemented by elapsed time.

The EMUs are inspected and maintained each 4,000 kilometers (km) or 48 hours, with mainly visual inspection and functional test (brakes, pantograph, toilet drainage, and cleaning), usually done overnight in the depot. In addition, whenever the EMUs enter or leave the EMU depot/workshop, lineside equipment tests every wheel.

Depot maintenance of varying degrees continues at intervals of from 20,000 to 800,000 km (broadly fortnightly to every two years) with the precise intervals depending on the type of rolling stock. This maintenance includes axle inspection, tread modification, gearbox oil change, bearing lubrication, and system and component function tests.

After this interval (that is, approximately 1.2 million km or three years) the EMUs undergo more extensive maintenance in either central depots or the manufacturing plant. This involves the bogies and tests the braking, traction, and air conditioning systems. At 2.4 million km, each of the main EMU systems (bogie, pantograph, brakes, motor and electrical performance testing, in-vehicle facilities, and paintwork) are stripped and repaired. Finally, at 4.8 million km or 12 years the entire vehicle is disassembled, replacing components, upgrading where necessary, and repainting.

Highlights

- Under the regulation and supervision of NRA, CRC is responsible for implementation of safety management through setting internal standards. It delegates the day-to-day implementation to the JVs and RAs throughout the construction phase and the operation phase.
- China manages safety risks throughout the project life cycle, by assuring appropriate technology in the design phase, quality construction in the building phase, and thorough inspection and maintenance in the operational phase.

- China collects asset condition data through a mix of physical inspection and dynamic testing with instrumented equipment. These data are analyzed centrally to identify maintenance requirements.
- During operation, a test train is run at the start of each day's operations to check the infrastructure. An instrumented train is run every 10 days to check condition.
- A four-hour window is provided every night for maintenance.

6 Finance

Before 2004, China's investment in high-speed rail (HSR) typically used the direct investment model. The Ministry of Railways (MOR) provided the funding for the investment and the local Regional Administration (RA) was responsible for implementing the project (figure 6.1).

Since 2004, most major projects have used the equity model. In this approach, the China Railway Corporation (CRC) through its subsidiaries such as China

FIGURE 6.1
Direct and equity financing models

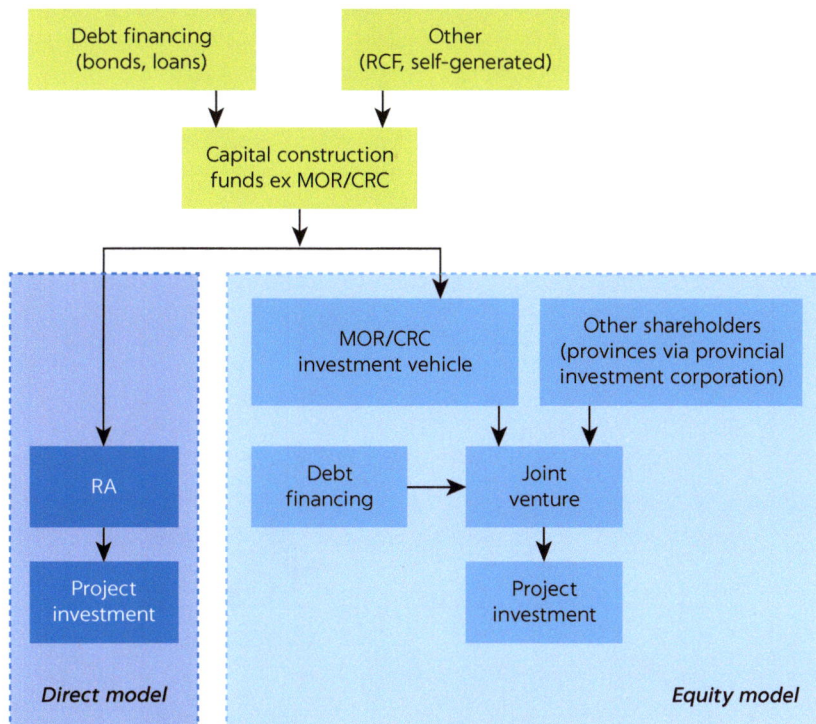

Note: CRC = China Railway Corporation; MOR = Ministry of Railways; RA = Regional Administration; RCF = Railway Construction Fund (which is funded by a surcharge on railway freight).

Railway Investment Corporation or the local RA forms a joint venture (JV) with local government (usually the provincial government),[1] sometimes with a small amount of third-party involvement, such as Ping An Insurance Group Co. of China Ltd. in the Beijing–Shanghai HSR company, China National Offshore Oil Corporation in the Beijing–Tianjin Intercity Railway Company, and Fosun Group in the Hangzhou–Shaoxing–Taizhou HSR company. Projects are typically financed with 50 percent equity from the JV partners and 50 percent loans from domestic banks (such as China Development Bank) and to a very limited extent from international banks.[2] CRC is largely responsible for implementing the project and mobilizing the financing. This approach is also called the "railway and local government cooperation" model.

This chapter analyzes four aspects of the financing of HSR projects:

1. Financial performance of the project companies
2. Overall financial performance of individual lines
3. Financial performance of the HSR network as a whole in China
4. How to make the finances more sustainable.

RA AND JV FINANCIAL PERFORMANCE

At present, there are two types of revenue models of JVs (figure 6.2). One is the ticket revenue model in which the JV takes revenue risk. In this model, the JV leases electric multiple units (EMUs) from the RA and contracts with the RA for train operations and infrastructure maintenance. The JV collects the revenue from passenger tickets and pays the RA for its services. The other model is the access charge model. In this model, the JV collects access charges for use of lines and stations by train operators and contracts with the RA for infrastructure maintenance. Access charges are set by CRC. The RA organizes the train service and retains the passenger ticket revenue, taking revenue risk. JV revenue and expenditure are primarily related to the number of trains operated rather than passenger volume. The board of directors of the JV chooses the model.

The access charge model, separating ownership and management, limits the options open to the asset owners to make the asset profitable, and restricts the attraction of HSR projects to private capital. However, it ensures the integrity of the network, with a unified transport organization, dispatching, and control. In principle, it would allow introduction of new operators in the future.

FIGURE 6.2
Ticket revenue and access charge models

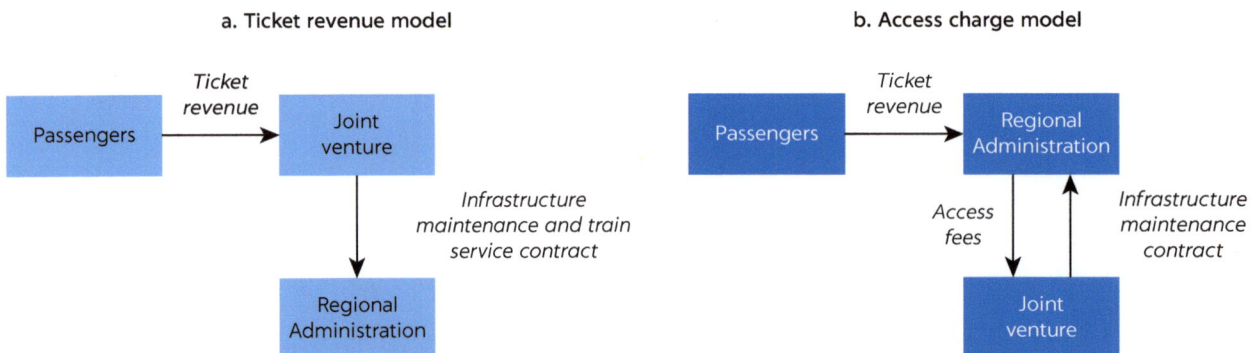

Transport safety is guaranteed by making full use of the equipment, personnel, and experience of the RAs, which maximizes the efficiency of the network, albeit at a cost of limiting innovation.

Except for a few JVs such as the Beijing–Shanghai HSR company, many now operate under the access charge model in which the JV is essentially an infrastructure financing and contract managing company and does not operate any services. These HSR JVs are analogous to tolled expressway companies—essentially asset management companies responsible for supervising construction, use, and maintenance of the asset and for debt service.

Table 6.1 summarizes the unit revenues and costs of the two main types of service.[3] Figure 6.3 and figure 6.4 translate these unit revenues and costs into financial results for the RA and JV. Figures 6.3 and 6.4 are both based on a 400 kilometer (km) line, with the 250-km-per-hour (kph) line having a traffic density[4] of 15 million passengers per year and the 350 kph line a density of 30 million passengers per year.

The RA experiences both higher revenue and higher train operating costs for the 350 kph services. Revenue per passenger-kilometer (pkm) is nearly 80 percent higher. Train operating costs are approximately 20 percent higher, mostly because of the difference in traction energy costs.[5] The capital cost of trainsets is nearly 50 percent higher for 350 kph relative to 250 kph; however, this difference is partly offset by the higher utilization the 350 kph trainset achieves (660,000 km per year compared to 440,000 km per year).

Considering both higher revenue and higher costs, 350 kph services in China earn three times more after train operating costs than 250 kph lines (Y 0.27 per pkm versus Y 0.09 per pkm). When translated into train-km earnings, 350 kph services earn Y 233.00/train-km versus Y 35.00/train-km for 250 kph services. This allows the RA to cover access charges from revenue for 350 kph services, but not for 250 kph services.

TABLE 6.1 China HSR unit revenues and costs, 2016

	UNITS	200–250 kph	300–350 kph
Passengers/train[a]	Passengers	390	825
Revenue[b]	Y/pkm	0.28	0.50
Train operating cost	Y/pkm	0.19	0.23
Net	Y/pkm	0.09	0.27
Net	Y/train-km	35	233
Access charge	Y/train-km[c]	70	153
Infrastructure maintenance cost	Million Y/km	1.80	2.30
Infrastructure investment cost	Million Y/km	110	130
Interest at opening[d]	Million Y/km	2.75	3.25
Principal repayment[d]	Million Y/km	2.75	3.25

Source: World Bank estimates.
Note: Train operating costs include the cost of electricity consumption of the electric multiple unit (EMU) trains, the repair and maintenance cost of the EMU trains, the salary of the crew, a share of the management cost, and the capital cost of the EMU trains (equivalent to about Y 0.05 per passenger-kilometer [pkm]). Fixed operating costs include infrastructure maintenance costs and a share of management costs. kph = kilometers per hour; Y = Chinese yuan.
a. Assumes 75 percent load factor.
b. Pkm based on number of passengers over 400 km line.
c. Charges are for an 8-car set for 200–250 line and for a 16-car set on 350 line. There is also a station access charge of Y 5.00 per passenger at large stations and less at smaller ones.
d. Based on 50 percent equity and 50 percent debt.

FIGURE 6.3

Costs and revenues, 250 kph line

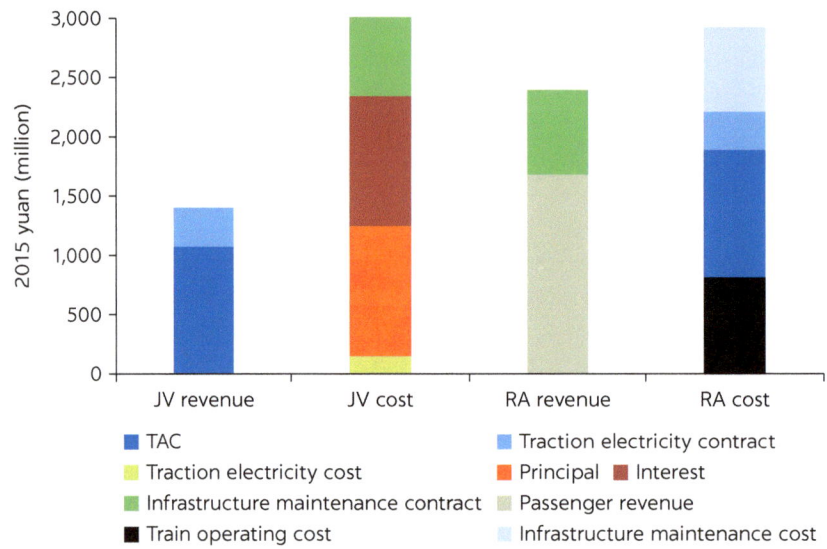

Source: Modeled on cost and revenue data in table 6.1.
Note: JV = joint venture; kph = kilometers per hour; RA = Regional Administration; TAC = track access charge.

FIGURE 6.4

Costs and revenues, 350 kph line

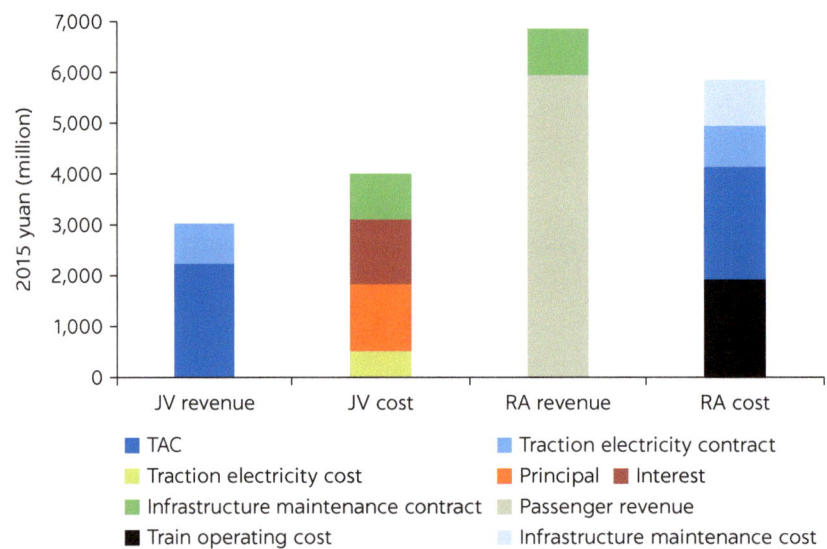

Source: Modeled on cost and revenue data in table 6.1.
Note: JV = joint venture; kph = kilometers per hour; RA = Regional Administration; TAC = track access charge.

For the RA, both cost and revenue directly vary with volume. The substantial difference in price between services causes the 350 kph services to be significantly more financially sustainable to the RA than the 250 kph services.

The JV receives revenue from access charges and incurs costs for infrastructure maintenance and debt service. In contrast to the RA, the JV's costs are largely fixed. However, its revenues vary with traffic volume, over which it has little control in practice.

The access charge is levied on a train-km basis. It is more than twice as high for a 350 kph line as for a 250 kph line, and the number of trains operated on a

350 kph line is usually greater as well. Maintenance cost per km is about 28 percent greater for a 350 kph line. Debt service is modeled as 50 percent debt and 50 percent equity, with an interest rate of 5 percent and a maturity of 20 years. The capital cost of a 350 kph line is about 18 percent higher than the 250 kph line, translating into higher interest and principal payments.

The result for the modeled lines—with 15 million pkm per year for the 250 kph line and 30 million pkm for the 350 kph lines—is negative for both the JVs, but substantially more negative for the 250 kph JV. Over time, the interest charges on infrastructure debt will reduce as the principal is repaid, improving the financial viability of the JVs. Nonetheless, the 250 kph JVs will face significant financial challenges for the foreseeable future, unless demand grows significantly or the access charges are increased. The financial prospects are brighter for the 350 kph JVs. Some very high-volume lines are already profitable, although many are not.

To date, the cash shortfall of the infrastructure JVs has been funded indirectly by the shareholding RA (because it is not paid for the infrastructure maintenance it performs) or by CRC through the assumption of part of the debt service.

LINE FINANCIAL PERFORMANCE

The overall financial performance of these lines—considering the infrastructure JV and the RA together—is a key benchmark of financial viability of the investments. In this case, passenger revenue is compared to all costs, including train operating costs, infrastructure maintenance costs, and debt service. Figure 6.5 shows the traffic density needed for the revenue net of train operating costs to cover three key thresholds of infrastructure cost:

1. Infrastructure maintenance cost
2. Infrastructure maintenance cost + interest
3. Infrastructure maintenance cost + interest + principal.

FIGURE 6.5

Breakeven passenger density at opening

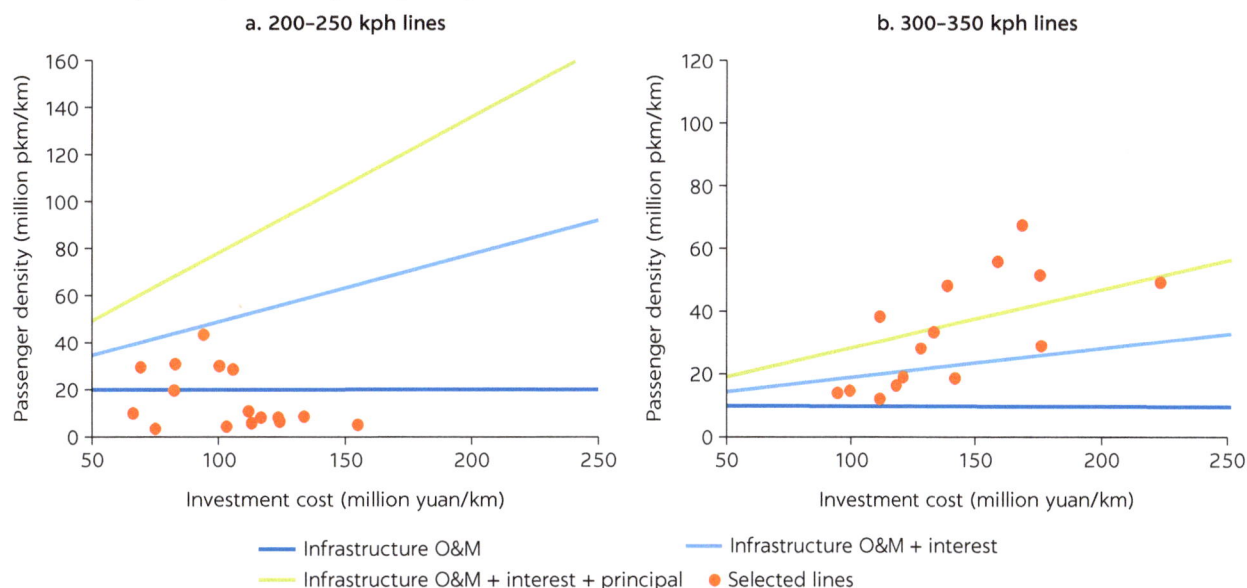

Source: Modeled on cost and revenue data in table 6.1.
Note: kph = kilometers per hour; O&M = operating and maintenance; pkm = passenger-kilometer.

The threshold densities have been calculated as of the opening date of a line, using the cost and revenue data of table 6.1. They are shown over a range of investment costs. The financing cost of the investment assumes 50 percent debt, with a 5 percent interest rate and a 20-year loan tenor. In figure 6.5, the dark blue line represents the annual maintenance cost. This is assumed to be constant, because it is essentially independent of the original investment cost, at least over the short and medium term. The other two lines are directly related to the size of the investment.

The lines compare different levels of cost coverage to the traffic volumes needed to achieve the cost coverage. The orange dots show the actual 2016 traffic densities for sixteen 250 kph projects and fifteen 350 kph projects. If a dot is above a line, the project's passenger revenues can cover the cost represented by the line.

Only five 200–250 kph lines are above the dark blue line, showing that they can cover their operating and maintenance costs. None of them is above the light blue line—that is, able to pay interest.[6] The primary reason for this is the low fare, which had little adjustment since 2007. In 2016, CRC was given authority to adjust fares on lines with speeds higher than 200 kph and has adjusted fares in many such cases.

The situation with the 300–350 kph HSR lines is more promising. All can cover their operating and maintenance costs. Nine out of the 15 lines can pay interest, and 5 of the eastern lines can repay the loan principal.

A significant percent of the traffic on these profit-making 300–350 kph lines, however, originates from the less profitable 200–250 kph lines. Therefore, a network approach may be taken when considering the financial performance.

The debt service on which the above analysis is based is for the opening year of operation, when the debt service amount is at its largest and demand is still developing. Over time, debt service will steadily reduce, partly because of repayments and partly because inflation will reduce its real cost.[7] Figure 6.6 shows the required volume to service debt at five-year intervals, based on a loan period of 20 years, and assuming an annual inflation rate of 2 percent.

The passenger volume needed for full payment of the debt service reduces year by year, so that 10 years after opening, 8 out of the 15 300–350 kph lines can pay their debt service in full just on today's volumes. The situation of the 200–250 kph lines, however, remains challenging. With the pre-2016 rates, only one or two 250 kph lines have any hope of being able to repay the principal, even in 10 years' time, unless they treble or quadruple their current volumes. China has recognized the need to address the financial challenge created by such low prices for the 250 kph lines and is starting to adjust prices to improve cost coverage.

Table 6.2 shows the traffic densities[8] needed to cover maintenance costs, interest, and principal for the average investment costs shown in table 6.1.

TABLE 6.2 Breakeven traffic densities (million passengers per year) at opening

	200–250 kph	300–350 kph
Maintenance	21	9
Maintenance + interest	53	21
Maintenance + interest + principal	85	33

Note: kph = kilometers per hour.

FIGURE 6.6

Breakeven passenger density for full debt service for future years, 50 percent debt:50 percent equity

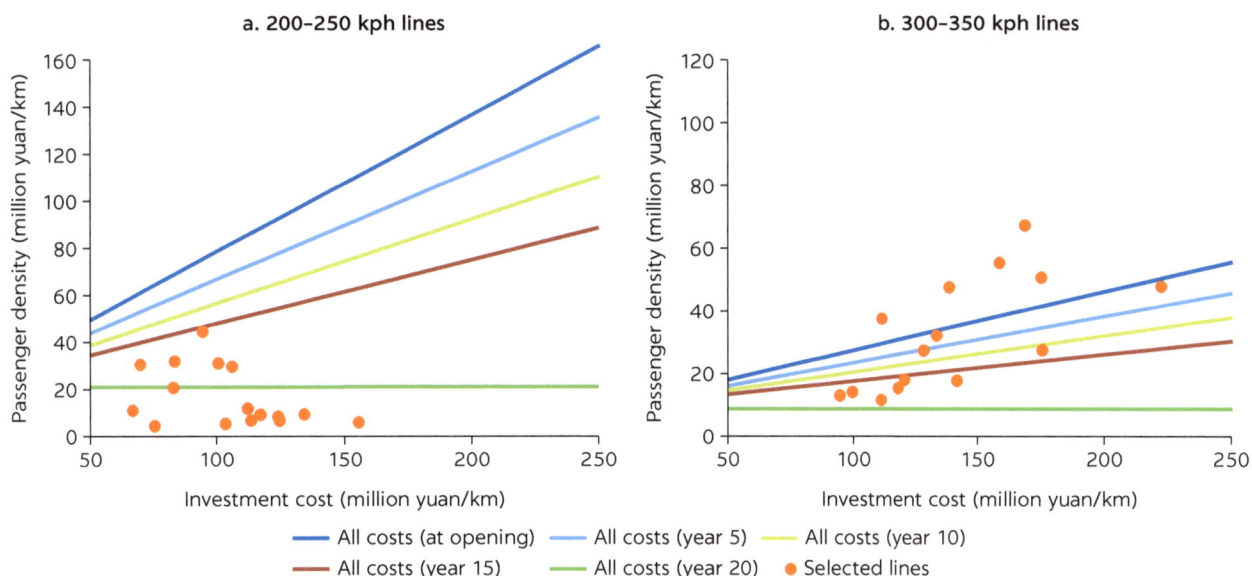

a. 200–250 kph lines

b. 300–350 kph lines

All costs (at opening) — All costs (year 5) — All costs (year 10) — All costs (year 15) — All costs (year 20) ● Selected lines

Source: Modeled on cost and revenue data in table 6.1.
Note: kph = kilometers per hour.

FIGURE 6.7

Breakeven tariffs for 250 and 350 kph lines, 50 percent debt:50 percent equity

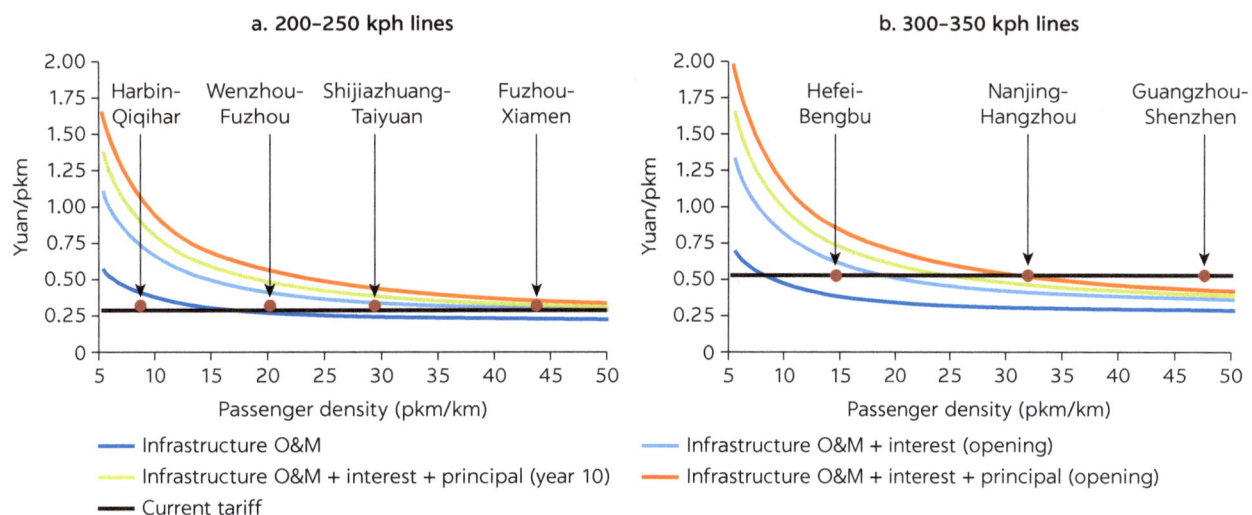

a. 200–250 kph lines

b. 300–350 kph lines

— Infrastructure O&M — Infrastructure O&M + interest (opening) — Infrastructure O&M + interest + principal (year 10) — Infrastructure O&M + interest + principal (opening) — Current tariff

Source: Modeled on cost and revenue data in table 6.1.
Note: kph = kilometers per hour; O&M = operating and maintenance; pkm = passenger-kilometer.

An alternative analysis is to derive the breakeven tariff for a given level of demand. Figure 6.7 shows this, assuming the average levels of investment given in table 6.1.

At current average revenue (Y 0.28/pkm [US$0.042/pkm]),[9] the 200–250 kph lines need passenger densities (within 10 years of opening) of 20 million to be able to cover infrastructure maintenance costs and another 30 million to cover the debt service.

The 300–350 kph lines, however, should be able to cover infrastructure maintenance at current average revenue levels per pkm. Traffic density of 20 million per year, which many but not all have, should allow them to also pay interest. Repayment of principal at that density would require a fare of Y 0.67/pkm (US$0.01/pkm). Only lines with traffic density of 35 million or more can cover full costs at the current fare level.

To place these traffic densities and fares in perspective, the Tokyo–Osaka line has a density of about 95 million passengers per year, with an average fare equivalent to Y 1.40 (US$0.021)/pkm; and the Taiwan, China HSR has a density of 31 million passengers per year, with a fare equivalent to Y 0.84 (US$0.013)/pkm. The other two main Japanese lines (Tohuku and Sanyo) have traffic densities of about 35 million. No European HSR has a traffic density greater than 20 million. Many Chinese lines are second only to Tokyo–Osaka in terms of passenger density, and Chinese fares (especially for 250 kph lines) are well below those in other countries.

NETWORK FINANCIAL PERFORMANCE

Given the financial situation described above, what is the result for the system as a whole? This section presents a consolidated forecast of the financial HSR-related costs and revenues for CRC and 100 percent of its subsidiary project companies for all HSR lines built as of December 31, 2015 (tables 6.3 and 6.4). It includes the construction and maintenance costs of the China Rail Highspeed (CRH) network and the revenue and cost of the CRH services to show the financial returns of the HSR investment. To evaluate the full impact on CRC, the

TABLE 6.3 **Assumptions made in the financial evaluation of high-speed rail**

ITEM	ASSUMPTION
Framework	The evaluations consider the difference in each of these groups of costs between a "with-project" case, in which the high-speed rail (HSR) network at end-2015 is constructed, and a "without-project" case, in which the network is not constructed but instead the China Railway Corporation provides incremental capacity to respond to the (lower) increase in demand that would still have occurred if the HSR network were not constructed.
Methodology	The streams of costs are calculated for each year of the evaluation period, here taken as the construction (and partial operation) period from 2005 to 2015 and a thirty-year operating period from 2015 to 2045.[a] A financial internal rate of return (FIRR) has been calculated by applying a discounted cash flow to this stream of costs and benefits using a 7 percent discount rate.
Traffic growth	Traffic on the end-2015 China Rail Highspeed services is forecast to grow at 15 percent in 2015, at 6 percent in 2016, at 3 percent per year from 2017 to 2030, and at 2 percent per year thereafter, giving a forecast traffic for 2045 of 1,300 billion passenger-kilometers. This growth profile allows for a continuing ramp-up for the lines just recently opened before settling down to a growth close to the real (that is, net of inflation) growth in incomes.
Diversion from other modes	Initially based on current diversion patterns but modified for future years to take into account future changes in car and aviation use increase over time.
Capital cost	The infrastructure construction costs used are as summarized in chapter 4. The capital cost of the HSR rolling stock has been approximated by converting its capital costs to an equivalent cost per year (in the same way as a leasing company) and including it in the rail operating costs. The capital costs avoided on the conventional network are based on typical costs.
Operator revenues and costs	These have been expressed as unit rates per passenger-kilometer in all cases except for HSR infrastructure maintenance, which has been expressed as a cost per route-kilometer. The rail costs are independent of revenue, but for other modes operating cost has been assumed as 90 percent of average revenue. For car travel, the marginal operating cost has been taken as fuel cost plus toll cost plus half of the maintenance cost, with an average occupancy of two. They are all assumed to increase in line with annual inflation of 2 percent per year.

a. The basic HSR is still capable of many more years of life beyond that time and this is allowed for by including a credit for 20 years of continuing operation at the end of the period.

TABLE 6.4 **Financial analysis of CRH network as of end-2015**

	YUAN, BILLION
HSR network	
Construction	−3,498
Revenue	6,329
Train operating cost	−3,020
Infrastructure maintenance	−554
Total	−743
Conventional network	
Capital cost avoided	468
Revenue lost	−940
Train operating cost saved	940
Total	468
Residual value[a]	1,570
Combined total	1,295

Note: Values in table are in billions of 2015 Chinese yuan discounted at 7 percent. CRH = China Rail Highspeed; HSR = high-speed rail.
a. The (discounted) value of the network at the end of the 30-year evaluation period.

financial impacts of the conventional rail services avoided by shifting passengers to HSR must be considered. This analysis includes the revenues, operating costs, and construction costs that have been avoided on the conventional rail network.

The financial internal rate of return (FIRR), considering the HSR revenues and costs alone (excluding the residual value), is estimated at 5.5 percent over 30 years. However, when the costs and savings associated with the conventional rail network are included, the FIRR increases to 6.4 percent. When the residual value of the HSR network is included, the FIRR increases to 8.6 percent. If inflation is zero, this reduces to 5.0 percent. Over a shorter period than 30 years, the financial results are not as good, with an FIRR of 4.1 percent for an evaluation period to 2035 and −2.4 percent for an evaluation period to 2025.

Given their much greater unit revenue, the 350 kph services perform somewhat better than the network as a whole, with an FIRR at 9.7 percent. Conversely, the 200–250 kph network has an FIRR of only 0.2 percent; the 9.5 percent disparity between it and the 300–350 kph lines is due to both the reduced unit revenue (5.7 percent) and the lower passenger density (3.8 percent).

FINANCIAL SUSTAINABILITY OF CHINA'S HSR

From 2005 onward, about Y 2.5 trillion (US$370 billion) was invested in the HSR network in service at end-2015. This was financed from a combination of the equity contribution from MOR/CRC and local governments, bank loans taken by the JVs (mostly from the major national and provincial development banks), central budget, and construction bonds of various types to finance the MOR/CRC equity contribution. The local government contributed land acquisition and resettlement, as well as support for material supply, facilities, and relief from local taxes. In some cases, private capital was also mobilized.[10]

The construction of HSR faces enormous financial pressure; to address this pressure China has developed a series of investment promotion policies, which are gradually being implemented. The basic strategy is to encourage the construction and operation of railways by private capital through promoting structures such as sole proprietorship and joint ventures, as well as the ownership and management rights. The public–private partnership model can also be used to attract investment by combining transport revenue and related development revenue. This model appears to be having some success with the more promising lines: Jinan to Qingdao is the first HSR line based on local government capital, and Hangzhou to Taizhou is the first HSR line financed over 51 percent by private capital.

At the more macro level, a railway development fund has been developed that combines seed capital from the central government with investments by long-term investors wanting a stable and reasonable return. Support will also be given for eligible enterprises to raise funds with corporate bonds and debt financing instruments, and permit major projects to issue renewable bonds. Financial institutions can also support the construction of railway projects through lending against assets such as mineral rights and franchises.

Nonetheless, financial sustainability and the ability to earn returns high enough to attract equity investment remain challenging. HSR lines with much passenger traffic need not worry about long-term financial problems. On many lines, however, revenue can cover the operation of the services but is insufficient to maintain the infrastructure. Currently the shareholding RAs have to partially absorb the cost of maintaining the infrastructure on these lines from their other operations. Only in rare cases do such lines cover even part of debt service.

A significant financial threshold for a railway is its ability to repay the principal on its loan. For many years it was commonly considered that only the Tokyo–Osaka and Paris–Lyon HSR lines have been able to reach this milestone. The busiest Chinese lines seem well on the way to also achieving it now, but for others it seems likely that repayment of principal will ultimately need to be rescheduled in one way or another.

A final financial threshold is earning high enough returns to attract equity investment. At current HSR fare levels, only the 350 kph lines with a density of over 35 million passengers are profitable enough to reach this level.

HOW TO ADDRESS FINANCING ISSUES

The options for addressing the HSR financing issues include

- Improving financial returns through increasing revenue, providing government subsidies, and reducing costs; and
- Restructuring debt by grouping lines and by reprofiling principal repayment.

Many of these mechanisms are already being employed and could be developed further and used in combination.

Increasing revenue. HSR fares may be adjusted to reflect market conditions. Passenger rail fares in China are determined by the government; however, in 2015 China liberalized the fares on new railway passenger lines financed by private capital, and in 2016 those on lines with speeds of more than 200 kph, which are wholly owned or held by CRC. HSR fares can now be independently adjusted on an individual basis depending on operation cost, market demand, competition, and social acceptability. The first line to do this was the Ningbo–Shenzhen section of the 200 kph Coastal Railway. This line is well-patronized (a density of over 30 million passengers) and well-developed, and average fares were increased by over 23 percent. This policy of adjusting fares to reflect local market conditions could improve the financial results of many lines and is especially important for 250 kph lines, whose low fares contribute to unsustainable finances. In the current situation, there is room for adjusting fares.

China HSR has already been trying to broaden its sources of revenue. Advertising, parcels, and station and on-train businesses are well-established. Land development also holds promise. HSR stations and surrounding areas should form part of a comprehensive land development plan. This type of planning will not only improve railway revenue but also encourage coordination between the layout of the railway station and external transport, city roads, and public transport.

Reducing costs. On the cost side, rail transport companies in China receive preferential tax treatment, with the first three years of operations being exempt from enterprise income tax under certain conditions and the next three years having tax reduced by 50 percent. Interest on railway bonds receives preferential tax treatment, and CRC continues to enjoy the preferential tax policies of the state toward the former MOR, as well as concessions from local governments.

Providing government subsidy. Once these possibilities have been exhausted, government subsidy is undoubtedly a direct and simple solution. After CRC was established in 2013, the State Council required CRC to establish an explicit mechanism for subsidies for rail passenger transport and studied ways of using financial subsidies to compensate for passenger service losses. As an interim measure to support railway reform, the central government implemented a transitional passenger traffic subsidy to CRC. In addition, for some railway projects controlled by private capital, the investment from the central government's dedicated fund may be supported by interest discounts and investment subsidies. Where projects with public welfare benefits are undertaken by private capital, there should be a reasonable compensation system. However, these policies need careful design to also encourage operators to increase transport revenue and control operating cost.

Grouping lines. HSR lines could be organized into a few large groups so that the main lines can support their feeder branches. Doing so does not change the underlying financial fundamentals but does enable more profitable lines to support less profitable lines. It is a reasonable approach, because up to 30 percent of traffic on the main lines originates from or is destined to those feeder lines.

Debt reprofiling. HSR debt may be restructured to extend the tenor of the loans or backload principal repayment to better match the growth in demand over time. Debt service pressure on HSR projects is largest at the start of operations and the commencement of principal repayment. Passenger demand is still developing, but principal repayment is large. Alternative debt schedules can better match the profile of repayments to the profile of cash generated by the project by putting more principal repayment at the end of the loan.

Highlights

- Some heavily used 350 kph lines are able to generate enough ticket revenue to pay for train operations, maintenance, and debt service. These are all lines with average traffic densities of 40 million+ passengers per year and average revenue per pkm of Y 0.5 (US$0.075).
- Many lines in China with traffic density of 10 million to 15 million passengers per year, especially 250 kph lines with revenue per pkm of Y 0.28 (US$0.042), can barely cover train operations and maintenance, and will be unable to contribute toward their debt service costs for many years unless their fares are significantly increased.
- These results should not be interpreted as demonstrating that 350 kph lines are inherently more financially viable than a comparable 250 kph line. The main reason by far is the pricing policy that has been adopted in China. For many low-medium corridors, a 250 kph line will be cheaper to build and more economical to operate, with probably only 10–15 percent less traffic than a comparable 350 kph line at the same fare levels.
- Options to improve cost coverage for loss-making lines include (i) increasing fares for 250 kph lines, where traffic demand permits, (ii) increasing nonfare revenue, and (iii) providing government subsidy.
- Financial restructuring options include (i) grouping feeder lines with main lines to pool revenues and costs and (ii) reprofiling principal repayment to shift payments to later years when traffic volumes are greater.

NOTES

1. Many provinces have established a Provincial Railway Investment Corporation, which invests in any rail projects within the province.
2. CRC finances its equity investments from its balance sheet. Its capital structure includes some Y 4 trillion of long-term debt.
3. The parameter values are consistent with the data used in China for HSR financial and economic evaluations. They are average values and individual lines will vary slightly.
4. Traffic density is measured as the sum of the traffic volume in each direction, measured as passenger-kilometers (pkm)/km of line.
5. The traction electricity charge covers both the electricity itself and the cost of the infrastructure that supplies it.
6. Based on the results obtained from the average costs. In practice, the situation of each line is slightly different.
7. Ticket prices and costs are growing by 2 percent a year, but loan principal and interest are unaffected.
8. The density of passenger flow is the total of the two directions.
9. Average revenue per pkm allows for the discounted fares for students, elderly, and other groups.
10. China National Offshore Oil Corporation has taken a 19 percent share in the Beijing–Tianjin line, and the Ping An Insurance Group Co. of China Ltd. has taken a 14 percent share in the Beijing–Shanghai line.

7 Economics

High-speed rail (HSR) has had wide-ranging impacts beyond the railway sector itself. More people are now able to travel more easily and reliably than before, and airlines and bus operators have had to change their service patterns on many routes. HSR has been a catalyst for changed patterns of urban development in many cities and has also led to substantial increases in tourism. Finally, it has provided the foundation for future savings in greenhouse gas (GHG) emissions.

An economic evaluation considers the costs[1] and benefits to society rather than to an individual organization. It includes not only the costs and benefits incurred by the railway but also those incurred by other transport operators such as airlines and bus companies. It also includes the costs and benefits to users in terms of the difference in travel time and ease of travel and to society as a whole in terms of externalities such as road accidents, congestion, and GHGs.

The World Bank has undertaken an indicative economic evaluation of the HSR program for those lines that were in service as of December 31, 2015. This is a preliminary estimate, because many of the lines have been open only for one or two years and the full influence of regional impacts will take several years to fully materialize. Nevertheless, the general pattern of the changes is becoming clear, and an economic evaluation is a useful tool for summarizing the various effects.

These effects can be summarized in five broad groups of costs and benefits:

1. Capital costs
2. Operator costs and benefits (all modes)
3. User costs and benefits
4. Externalities (that is, costs and benefits to third parties, principally GHG emissions, road congestion, and road accidents)[2]
5. Regional economic development.

The economic evaluation builds on the assumptions used in chapter 6 for the financial evaluation (table 6.1) with additional assumptions on user costs and benefits and externalities (table 7.1). As shown in box 7.1, the economic rate of return varies across lines.

TABLE 7.1 Assumptions made in the economic evaluation of high-speed rail

ITEM	ASSUMPTION
Operator revenues and costs	These have been expressed as unit rates per passenger-kilometer in all cases except for high-speed rail (HSR) infrastructure maintenance, which has been expressed as a cost per route-kilometer. The rail costs are independent of revenue, but for other modes operating cost has been assumed as 90 percent of average revenue. For car travel, the marginal operating cost has been taken as fuel cost plus toll cost plus half of the maintenance cost, with an average occupancy of 2. These costs are the same as in table 6.1 but exclude inflation (because all calculations are done in real terms).
User benefits and costs	The value of time (VOT) for business travel has been assumed equal to the wage rate with that for nonbusiness travel taken as one-third of the wage rate. This value has been combined with income data collected in the onboard surveys (see chapter 3) and assumed (see chapter 6) to grow over time in line with income. Improvements in service quality have been allowed for by a 10 percent uplift in the VOT used for HSR services.
Greenhouse gas emissions	Converted to money terms in the economic evaluation using the 2015 World Bank economic price for carbon dioxide of US$30 per ton, increasing to US$50 per ton (in real terms) by 2045.
Road congestion	Calculated indirectly as the lane-km required to maintain the same level of congestion as in the no-HSR case, using a construction cost per lane-km of Y 2 million (US$300,000).
Road accidents	Road accident rates per vehicle-km assumed to fall by 2 percent per year, combined with a Value of Statistical Life of 50 times GDP per capita, increasing over time as GDP increases.
Regional development	Twenty percent of the above benefits, based on a range of studies in other countries.

BOX 7.1

Economic returns for China's high-speed rail

The World Bank has financed parts of six high-speed rail projects in China. Postproject evaluation for the four completed projects show positive economic returns (table B7.1.1).

TABLE B7.1.1 Economic rate of return

LINE	ECONOMIC RATE OF RETURN (%)
Shijiazhuang–Zhengzhou	15
Guiyang–Guangzhou	18
Jilin–Hunchun	8
Nanning–Guangzhou	16

CAPITAL COSTS

The China Railway Corporation (CRC) incurs capital costs for both infrastructure (chapter 4) and rolling stock (chapter 6). CRC also receives benefits as the additional capacity provided by the HSR construction, and the consequent diversion of passenger demand (and passenger services) from the conventional network to HSR, which allows the postponement of capacity expansion that would otherwise be required on the conventional network.

OPERATOR COSTS AND BENEFITS

Operator costs and benefits include the changes in revenue and marginal operating costs for each mode as a result of the changes in demand. The unit rates (table 6.1) are combined with the demand forecasts to provide operator costs by mode by year. Operator revenue can be similarly calculated; it is equal and opposite to user fare costs.

USER COSTS AND BENEFITS

User costs and benefits cover the difference in user cost, time, and convenience between the "with-project" case and the "without-project" case. User costs are straightforward, being the fares paid to operators both on the railway itself and on access modes.

User time savings are those incurred by HSR users compared to the time they would have spent using their "without-project" modes. These savings also need to consider differences in access and egress time between the airports, stations, and bus terminals and the users' ultimate origins and destinations.

The time savings can be converted into money terms using what is known as the value of time (VOT). This is the value that users put on changes in the time it takes them to make a particular trip, on which there is an extensive literature. VOT is generally assumed to be a function of income, reflecting that those with higher incomes tend to use the modes with the shortest travel times.

In addition to cost and time, users also experience benefits from the improved level of service provided by HSR in terms of comfort, reliability, service frequency, and ease of purchasing a ticket.

GREENHOUSE GAS EMISSIONS

Carbon emissions[3] associated with HSR arise throughout a project's life cycle, from planning and design through materials production, construction, operation and maintenance, and dismantling. The relative importance of these emissions critically depends on the volume of traffic. Emissions associated with construction are a function of the capacity provided, which may or may not be fully utilized; therefore, whereas operating emissions dominate on a high-density line, the reverse is true on a lower-volume line.

Carbon emissions during the planning and design stage are small in absolute terms compared with other stages. Vehicle manufacture also is a small part (about 3 percent) of the total vehicle-related emissions (Yue et al. 2015). However, HSR infrastructure construction consumes a large amount of material and energy. Most carbon emissions come from three sources: cement (50 percent), steel (30 percent), and fuel and energy (10 percent). Overall emissions for typical HSR lines range from about 25,000–35,000 tons of carbon dioxide per route-kilometer (km), depending on the proportion of bridges and tunnels. Emissions associated with demolition are much smaller, typically 2,000 tons per route-km.

During HSR operations, carbon emissions are dominated by the electric energy consumed for traction (80–90 percent of the total) and the energy consumed by the auxiliary facilities and equipment at stations and depots (10–20 percent of the total).

Traction energy consumption is primarily a function of speed, stopping patterns, and vehicle mass but is also affected by factors such as grade.[4] HSR electric multiple units (EMUs) generally adopt streamlined bodies, lightweight technology, and regenerative braking, all of which help reduce energy consumption.

Electricity usage by itself does not generate carbon emissions; these emissions are produced during power generation. The average national carbon emission index in China, taken across all methods of generation, is currently 0.98 kilogram per kilowatt-hour (kg/kWh),[5] which gives a range for HSR emissions from train operation of 35–60 kg per 1,000 passenger-km (pkm), depending on speed and line, based on an average occupancy of 75 percent.

The total GHGs emitted over the life of an HSR project is thus a function of the passenger density (figure 7.1). For the busiest lines such as Beijing–Shanghai, with densities of over 50 million passengers per year, about 90 percent of lifetime emissions come from operations; but this proportion drops to 60 percent for lower-volume lines with 10 million to 20 million passengers per year.[6]

Because of its higher speed, an HSR uses considerably more energy, and thus generates more CO_2/pkm than a conventional electric railway, typically

FIGURE 7.1

GHG per pkm as a function of passenger density

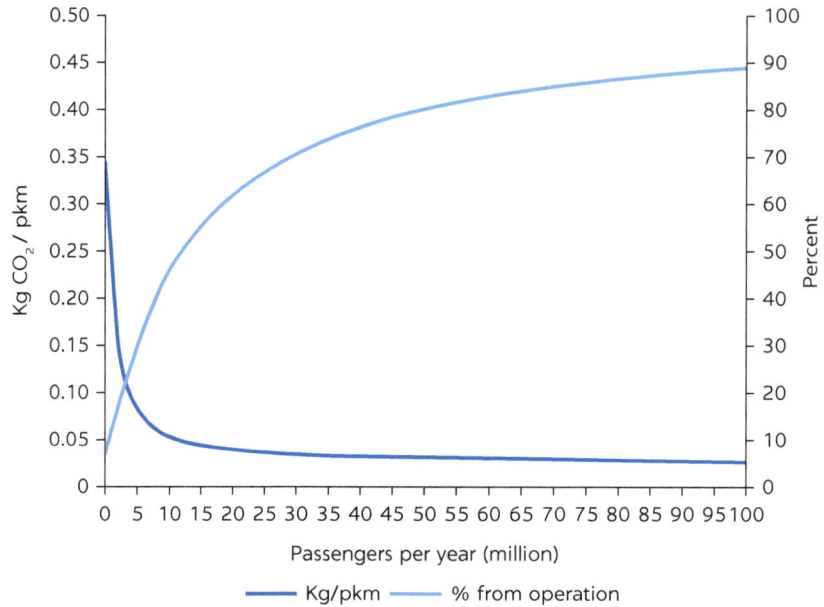

Note: Figure assumes 32,000 tonnes per kilometer for construction and demolition, 0.045 kilograms (kg) per passenger-kilometer (pkm), and a life of 100 years. GHG = greenhouse gas.

about double. Its emissions are, however, about one-third to one-half those of aircraft.[7]

About half the HSR passengers in 2015 are estimated to have transferred from conventional rail services and a further 20 percent from air. About 15 percent came from bus and car, and the remaining share was generated. The estimated net effect was a small reduction of about 2 percent in CO_2 emissions if the HSR network were not there. Over time, however, as emissions per kWh of electricity reduce and travel increasingly shifts from conventional rail to air and car, this reduction should increase to about 60 percent.

In the future, HSR in China may also have an indirect effect on reducing carbon emissions by providing more capacity for freight on the conventional railway, which has significant energy saving and emission reduction compared with other freight land transport modes.

ROAD CONGESTION AND ACCIDENTS

HSR attracted an estimated 15 percent of its passengers in 2015 from roads for short- and medium-distance trips. This switch reduces both congestion and accidents on these roads. An extra 1,500 lane-km on the main road networks would have been needed in the absence of HSR to be able to provide the same level of service as was actually achieved.[8]

Reliable data on Chinese highway accident rates are difficult to find but in 2006–08 the estimated fatality rate on the expressways was about 21 per billion vehicle-km, based on the police data. This is a very high rate,[9] but experience in other countries has been that these rates reduce as motorization increases. Allowing for this, the HSR network saved an estimated 140 lives from highway accidents in 2015.

As with GHGs, the number of fatalities needs to be expressed in money terms to be used in the economic evaluation. This is conventionally done using what is termed the Value of Statistical Life (VOSL). VOSL is normally obtained by surveys, but most results show a close relationship to gross domestic product per capita, with VOSL typically being 40–70 times larger. A value of 50 has been assumed in this evaluation.

In future years there will be further savings in congestion and road accidents, directly related to the annual increase in passengers diverted from car and bus.

HSR AND ECONOMIC DEVELOPMENT

In addition to its direct economic benefits, HSR has played an important role in promoting regional economic and macroeconomic development. The HSR services have generated many new trips, for both business and leisure. The business trips are in principle associated with the development of larger and better-connected markets, which in turn should promote regional development for the areas served by the new services. Interviews with both passengers and businesses confirm that HSR services have significantly increased mobility and interaction between urban centers (box 7.2).

With about 50 percent of riders traveling for business purposes, for a total ridership of 1.7 billion passengers per year, over 850 million new opportunities are created to connect, trade, and exchange ideas each year—compared to the situation prior to the HSR—leading to additional economic activity, innovation, and increased productivity.

In almost all feasibility studies, national and provincial governments stress the importance of transport influencing regional economic development.[10] Studies have also shown that transport improvements can stimulate economic activity if they can materially improve accessibility, especially to major national and regional hubs of commerce and information. All else being equal, a new business located within daily reach of such hubs will be more accessible to a larger pool of labor and other businesses, raising productivity (U.K. Department for Transport 2005). This result is an important element of what are broadly referred to as agglomeration economies, the benefits that accrue to firms and individuals from the clustering of economic activity. HSR greatly shortens the time between different regions, thus encouraging such interactions and improving productivity. People, logistics, and information can flow faster and more conveniently over a wider area; and there is a better allocation of resources such as talent, capital, and technology and a better match of production and consumption, thus driving economic growth.

China is at a turning point in its urbanization[11] and in 2014 issued a national urbanization plan to 2020. Small and medium-sized centers—often with only a single main industry, restricting the development of the city—have experienced a continuous loss of talent to large centers. Large cities, by contrast, have high population densities, lack of space, and environmental problems, all affecting business efficiency. HSR aims to reverse this situation by providing a transport backbone that will stimulate complementarity between its cities and allow talent and technology to be devolved to smaller centers to improve their overall competitiveness. These cities will seek to develop their secondary and service industries, and their competitiveness will be strongly influenced by the quality of their transport connections to national and international supply chains and

BOX 7.2

Case study: The impact of high-speed rail on businesses

A series of business interviews were conducted in 2013 and 2015 in four cities with newly built high-speed rails (HSRs) (Changchun, Jilin, Jinan, and Tianjin), together with centers along the Guiguang, Nanguang, and Shizheng HSR corridors. The objective was to understand how businesses and individuals use HSR, and how this use has modified their patterns of work and daily life as well as business decision making. Key points from the interviews include the following:

- *Site selection by enterprises*: Manufacturing businesses do not consider HSR as a significant factor in site selection. The key influences are government preferential policies, land availability, and general traffic conditions, encouraging moves to new economic zones. Some smaller enterprises engaged in professional services and logistics take into account the convenience of intercity travel, but in general the influence of HSR on site selection is relatively low.

- *Business operations*: Most manufacturing enterprises consider that HSR has significantly influenced business travel because it lowers travel expenses, saves time, and improves productivity. Sales, procurement, and professional service staff now rely heavily on HSR for business trips (typically three to six per month). Service companies can now cover neighboring centers more easily, improving staff allocation,

broadening catchment areas, and allowing faster responses.

- *Personal lives*: HSR appears to have intensified interurban integration. Family and social interactions have become more frequent, often bringing business opportunities. In many cities (for example, Tianjin West and Zhengzhou East), the opening of the HSR station has been a major force driving real estate residential development.

- *Local tourism and recreational industries*: HSR benefits tourism in three ways. First, HSR tickets are relatively easy to get, which makes it easier to arrange tourist itineraries. Second, HSR significantly shortens the time spent traveling, thus permitting weekend trips that were impossible before. Third, HSR offers a clean and comfortable ride, which is favored by tourists and makes HSR the first choice for trips shorter than 500 km.[a]

In summary, HSR has had a marked impact on the mobility of local businesses and the personal mobility of their staff. This effect has brought about not only increased sales and productivity but also increased social opportunities. It has had little significant influence on business location but has facilitated the setting up of new regional branches, particularly in professional services, and is encouraging tourism along the HSR corridors.

a. An interesting side effect is that, because of the better accessibility and reliability of HSR, the period of prior ticket sales for many events has been shortened from one and a half months to one month, catchment areas have been increased, and audiences can now travel independently instead of requiring organized transport.

innovation networks. This is recognized in the Medium- and Long-Term Railway Plan through the rapid rail network.

One of the biggest challenges faced by China remains the impoverished areas with their generally poor populations. China is thus seeking to rebalance its growth geographically to reduce poverty and enhance inclusiveness. After three decades of rapid development in eastern China, the development of the central and western provinces is now a prime objective of Chinese policy. An important government policy is "traffic poverty alleviation," using HSR to link the economic activities of all regions into a whole, so the economically developed regions can drive the development of economically backward regions. A recent econometric study has found that "a positive impact of HSR on promoting regional economic convergence in China is confirmed through the panel regression analysis after controlling for other key factors, including capital investment, globalization, marketization, education and fiscal decentralization" (Chen and Haynes 2019, 172).

URBAN DEVELOPMENT

The massive development of HSR goes hand in hand with the massive development of new urban areas, especially in small to medium-sized cities. The municipal government often put the new HSR station in an undeveloped area and bundled it with an urban development plan of the "HSR new town." This model brought the municipal government significant fiscal revenues through land sales to real estate developers. There are at least 139 cities with at least one HSR new town in China (Chen and Haynes 2019). Chen and Haynes's study showed that the development of the HSR station contributes to about 3–13 percent of land value increase of the nearby area, and the effect is stronger if the land is closer to the HSR station.

The outcome of such urban development associated with new HSR lines and stations, however, varies among cities. With integrated urban development around the new stations, some HSR new towns, such as Bengbu, turned into vibrant urban spaces. Meanwhile, many others failed because of the isolation from existing urban areas, lack of public infrastructure, and the oversupply of real estate properties.

TOURISM

Although most HSR travel is undertaken by residents along the line, such patterns do not hold when the center served by the improved service is a major tourist attraction, for which the bulk of travelers will be based in other cities (box 7.3). This recreational tourism is a discretionary activity, which is undertaken or not depending on competing tourist attractions or of alternative ways of spending discretionary income. This freedom of choice means it is much more sensitive to changes in the cost of travel. It is also sensitive to the ease of travel; many of these trips are typically done over a weekend or a short holiday period (such as a three-day weekend). Changes in the accessibility of a tourist location in terms of travel time (for example, being able to complete a round trip as well as spend a reasonable amount of time at the destination) and in the ease of obtaining tickets for travel (many of such trips are made at comparatively short notice, often subject to short-term influences like the weather) have a major influence on recreational travel behavior.[12]

ECONOMIC RATE OF RETURN

Table 7.2 and figure 7.2 summarize the results of this analysis.

User time savings are the largest single contributor to the project benefits, but operating cost savings and externalities (including regional development benefits) together represent about 30 percent. GHG benefits are negative because the operating period of the analysis is not long enough to overcome the substantial GHG embedded in the construction. The economic rate of return is estimated at 8 percent, a good result for such a large investment.

BOX 7.3

Case study: High-speed rail and tourism in Qufu

Qufu, in Shandong about 500 kilometers (km) south of Beijing and about 800 km north of Shanghai, was the home of Confucius and has been an important center for Chinese travelers for many hundreds of years. It now receives large numbers of tourists, particularly during the summer months. In 2010, 1.4 million tickets were sold at Confucius Temple, the main attraction and a good proxy for the total number of tourists attracted to Qufu.

Before the opening of the Beijing–Shanghai high-speed rail (HSR) line, relatively few tourists came by rail to Qufu itself because of low frequencies, long travel times from the main tourist generators (Beijing, Shanghai, Nanjing), and inconvenient times. Such tourists who did use rail generally traveled to neighboring major centers and then toured the region by bus; a weekend trip to Qufu from major centers was open only to the very determined.

The introduction of the HSR has provided a completely new market. The new HSR station handled 2.6 million passengers in 2012 and 3.5 million in 2013. About 30 percent of the 2013 passengers traveled to and from Beijing, about 12 percent to and from Shanghai, and about 6 percent to and from Nanjing. Clearly such a large number cannot only be tourists, but equally tourists must have contributed significantly. Group tours now connect from HSR to bus; as a result, about 30 percent of group tours (about 110,000 visitors) are now booked through local tour operators compared to 12 percent before the HSR opened. The proportion of independent visitors has increased from 70 percent to about 80 percent. Ticket sales for the Confucius Temple increased by 10 percent immediately after the HSR opened, with much higher increases achieved from the limited number of cities that were directly connected by the HSR at that time.

The hotel industry has responded by building additional accommodations. Prior to the opening of the HSR, Qufu had about 11,000 beds in some 329 hotels; 11 of these (with just over 2,000 beds) were "starred" hotels. About 30 new hotels opened from the second half of 2010 to 2013, providing over 3,000 new beds; and in 2013 several further hotels, with 1,000 new beds, were under construction, including two new five-star hotels.

TABLE 7.2 **Economic costs and benefits by component**

	BENEFITS
Construction cost	−3,367
Rail construction deferred	442
User time savings	2,209
Operating cost savings	889
Infrastructure maintenance	−465
Generated traffic benefits	473
GHG benefits	−126
Accident savings	2
Road congestion savings	9
Regional benefits	596
Total	662

Note: Values in table are in billions of 2015 Chinese yuan discounted at 7 percent. GHG = greenhouse gas.

Indicative results for the two types of line are that the 350 kph lines have an economic internal rate of return (EIRR) of about 9 percent (including regional benefits) and the 250 kph and below lines have an EIRR of about 6 percent. This difference is not as marked as might be thought because the difference in unit revenue, a key factor in any financial analysis, does not enter the economic analysis because it is a transfer payment between users and operators.

FIGURE 7.2

Economic costs and benefits of high-speed rail

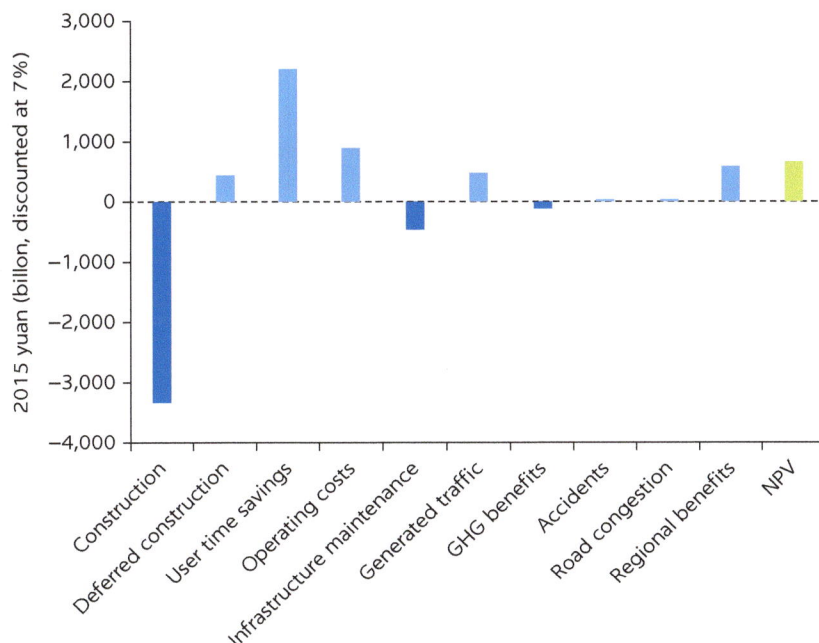

Note: GHG = greenhouse gas; NPV = net present value.

TABLE 7.3 **Sensitivity tests on EIRR**

	EIRR (%)
Base	8.0
Exclude regional benefits	6.8
50% of time savings	5.8
50% of operating cost savings	7.1
Exclude regional benefits/externalities	7.1

Note: EIRR = economic internal rate of return.

The rate of return is reasonably robust against a series of sensitivity tests on the key components (table 7.3).

The economic rate of return is, however, heavily dependent on the travel volume on the network. In 2015, the average network density was 23 million passengers. If the density of the CRC network had been only 15 million passengers, the EIRR would have reduced to about 5 percent, just economically viable by Chinese benchmarks. If the density reduces further, however, the EIRR declines sharply, and for a density of 5 million it has become negative. An EIRR of 0 percent is about 7 million passengers (figure 7.3). The traffic density in China is high compared to everywhere outside Japan and Taiwan, China.

These EIRR results are specific to the circumstances of the Chinese system. They are likely to be more favorable than in many other countries, given the relatively cheap construction costs, high passenger density by world standards, and efficient operations. The results are independent of the fare charged, because what is an economic benefit to the operator is an equal and opposite cost to the user, with the proviso that the higher the fare the lower the number of users and thus the lower their economic benefits.

FIGURE 7.3

EIRR sensitivity to passenger density

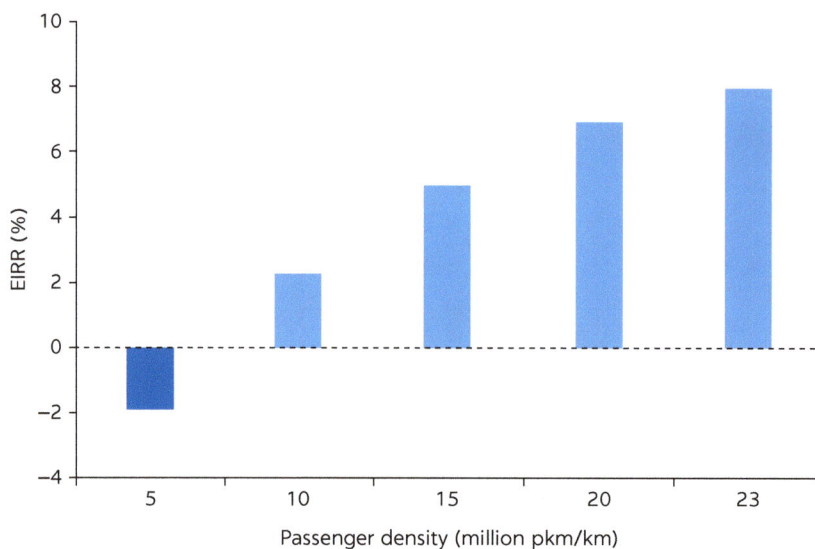

Note: EIRR = economic internal rate of return; pkm/km = passenger-kilometer/kilometer.

Highlights

- Economic benefits in China are dominated by user time savings (especially for those transferring from conventional trains and land modes) and by operator cost savings.
- The most significant ongoing externality benefit is from reduced GHG emissions, but this effect is relatively small and needs substantial volume to overcome the GHG emissions involved in the initial construction.

- Regional development impacts are already emerging, but their full impact will only be seen over a longer time period.
- In China, the HSR system as of end-2015 appears to be economically successful but returns for systems with lower traffic densities will be marginal or negative.

NOTES

1. These are strictly speaking economic costs and benefits; include adjustments where financial costs do not reflect the underlying economic costs—in short, "remove taxes and include subsidies." This was a significant problem in China in the days of the fully planned economy but is not currently a significant issue and has been ignored for the purposes of this analysis.
2. Although HSR does impose some costs on third parties through the need for land for the right-of-way, noise to adjacent settlements, and so on, these issues have been increasingly addressed through the much greater use of viaducts and tunnels to minimize land take and noise barriers in sensitive areas.
3. A range of gases contribute to GHGs, but these are not significant when analyzing rail operations, typically adjusting the impact of carbon dioxide (CO_2) alone by only 0.5 percent.
4. Grade is the most significant infrastructure factor influencing HSR energy consumption but is not a major factor in eastern China.

5. This is expected to reduce to under 0.50 kg/kWh over the next 30 years as the generation mix changes.

6. This result is specific to China. For a country like France, where the CO_2 emissions per kWh are about 10 percent of those in China, the balance between construction and operations is very different. The balance is also closely related to the assumed lifetime of the infrastructure.

7. After allowance is made for radiative forcing in the upper atmosphere.

8. Based on a lane capacity of 20,000 vehicle-km (vkm) per day (7.3 million vkm per year).

9. Comparable rates in developed countries for similar road networks are 4 to 7 per billion vkm.

10. This is often expressed using the concept of one- and two-hour travel circles—highlighting the change in a given city's economic hinterland before and after HSR.

11. In 2016, 57 percent of the population (790 million) was urbanized, but by 2030 this is expected to increase to 70 percent (about 1 billion).

12. A good example is the growth of what is called the "weekend break" market in Europe—often for two or three days. Such trips have only been made possible by the growth of cheap airlines and the introduction of easy self-ticketing on the Internet.

REFERENCES

Chen, Zhenhua, and Kingsley Haynes. 2019. *High Speed Rail and China's New Economic Geography*. Cheltenham, U.K., and Northampton, MA: Edward Elgar Publishing.

U.K. Department for Transport. 2005. "Transport, Wider Economic Benefits, and Impacts on GDP." Discussion Paper, U.K. Department for Transport, London.

Yue, Ye, Tao Wang, Sai Liang, Jie Yang, Ping Hou, Shen Qu, Jun Zhou, Xiaoping Jia, Hongtao Wang, and Ming Xu. 2015. "Life-Cycle Assessment of High Speed Rail in China." *Transportation Research Part D: Transport and Environment* 41 (December): 367–76.

8 Conclusions

Over the last decade, China has put into operation 25,000 kilometers (km) of dedicated high-speed railway (HSR) lines—far more than the rest of the world put together. China was the first country with a gross domestic product per capita below US$7,000 to invest in developing an HSR network. China's achievement in HSR is remarkable and worthy of study. China is unique in many ways, including size (9.6 million km^2), and substantial population density (141 people per km^2). China has many well-interspaced medium and large cities located at distances that are well suited for HSR. In the decade up to 2010—the formative years of HSR program planning—the number of Chinese cities with population greater than a quarter million increased from 376 to 451, and the number of very large cities (more than 5 million people) jumped from 59 to 82. This increase drove a need for investment in interurban transport connectivity and required a network solution. What of this experience is unique to China, and what is instructive for other countries considering investment in HSR?

Planning. Careful planning, consistently implemented, is required to deliver a large infrastructure program. In China, development of a well-analyzed Long-Term Plan provided a clear and consistent framework for action. Government provided strong support for the plan, and changes to the plan were minimal, which provided a strong framework upon which all parties could depend and focus on delivery.

Scale. Because of the massive scale of the investment program, China was able to develop an innovative and competitive supply industry for design and construction of high-speed infrastructure, systems, and rolling stock. It has standardized designs for many HSR components. This has contributed to infrastructure construction costs that are about 30 percent lower than in Europe. Although few countries will be able to match China's scale, they may gather some of the benefits of scale by using standard designs and tapping the competitive supply industry internationally.

Capacity. Capacity development is key to managing an HSR program. China started building capacity long before it started building the HSR network. China explored and adopted HSR technologies that were available internationally, improving and localizing technology over time. China invested heavily in engineering technology training and created an "ecosystem" of design institutes, universities, capable contractors, and capable railway staff to implement the program.

Local partnerships. Partnering with local government benefits the HSR program. China has delivered HSR infrastructure through a joint venture structure for implementation of HSR projects that secured local government support and financing for the projects.

Project management. China has a remarkable record of on-time, on-budget project delivery. Aspects of the project management system that contribute to this include project management structure with clear responsibilities and delegation of authority, managers who stay for the entire duration of the project, strong project logistics, and significant incentive compensation for managers.

Safety. A rigorous safety regime is necessary to deliver HSR safely. China's system manages safety risks throughout the project life cycle by assuring appropriate technology in the design phase, quality construction in the building phase, and thorough inspection and maintenance in the operational phase. This rigorous safety regime is replicable in any country; however, it depends on developing high capacity at all levels of the safety system.

Service. To be competitive, HSR service must operate with high punctuality, frequency, and speed. In China the HSR service has a punctuality rate of over 98 percent for departures and 95 percent for arrivals, with Fuxing trains having even better punctuality. Its minimum frequency is hourly service between 7:00 a.m. and midnight, and more than 70 train pairs are operated on busy routes. Line speed varies between 200 and 350 kilometers per hour (kph), depending on the line's role in the network, market demand, and engineering conditions with investment cost. In China, the attractiveness of the service is enhanced because it is a network with many HSR lines and interchanges with the conventional rail lines, allowing passengers to reach many locations by rail.

Markets. HSR is suited to medium-distance travel markets with very high travel demand. In China, HSR is very competitive with other modes for distances of 150–800 km (about three to four hours travel time), and the 350 kph service is competitive up to 1,200 km. For shorter distances, customers prefer bus and private automobile, and for longer distances customers prefer air. Achieving reasonable occupancy at a minimum service level (hourly between 7:00 a.m. and midnight) requires 4 million passengers per year, and achieving financial viability at Chinese costs and fares requires 40 million passengers per year. These figures may differ for other countries with different projects and pricing. Nonetheless, they indicate that HSR is not suitable for markets with low passenger volumes. Chinese geography, with many large cities within appropriate HSR travel distance, lends itself to HSR. Other countries may consider whether their population density pattern and distances are similarly suited.

Urban connectivity. HSR is more attractive to customers when well connected to the cities it serves. In China, HSR stations are often built outside the downtown area for cost and urban development reasons. This placement increases the cost to customers of HSR (in terms of both time and money) and reduces its competitiveness. Improving links to the urban transport system can help overcome this disadvantage. Integrated urban development around the new stations brings the economic benefits of HSR to the local community.

Pricing. HSR prices need to be set at levels that are competitive with other modes and affordable for the population. In China, HSR prices are about one-fourth of HSR prices in Europe, but three to four times the cost of conventional rail tickets in China—including the very cheap "hard seat" tickets that are a public service of the China Railway Corporation (CRC). HSR prices are low enough that a broad range of income groups patronize the high-speed trains, representing now more than half of all intercity rail passengers and 1.7 billion passenger trips in 2017. The strong growth in HSR traffic indicates that many consumers in China are willing to pay substantially more for a higher-quality service. Continued strong patronage of conventional services also indicates a continued strong demand for lower-cost/lower-quality services and the need to offer a range of services at different price points to meet different passenger needs.

Financial viability. A developing country can price HSR service affordably and still be financially viable. This financial viability, however, is strongly dependent on adequate traffic density and appropriate price. The lines in China that generate enough ticket revenue to pay for train operations, maintenance, and debt service have average traffic density of more than 40 million passengers per year and a price of Y 0.50 (US$0.075) per passenger-km. Lines that are priced lower require even higher traffic density to cover costs. Thus, the railway needs to seek the "sweet spot" in pricing that encourages high ridership but maximizes revenue generation and cost coverage. This strategy has started in China with increasing price flexibility being given to CRC.

Economic viability. HSR can be economically viable in a developing country. The HSR services have provided significant benefits to users in terms of reduced travel time and improved service quality. Economic benefits also accrue because of users of higher-cost modes such as air and automobile transferring to HSR, including external costs (accidents, road congestion, and greenhouse gases). Other economic benefits are associated with improved regional connectivity. HSR can contribute to rebalancing growth geographically to reduce income disparity. Analysis of the Chinese investment in HSR as of 2015 showed the economic rate of return to be positive; however, economic viability depends on high traffic density. Countries that anticipate lower traffic density or higher construction costs than China's, or both, will find financial and economic viability to be very challenging.

The Chinese HSR story is not complete. China is continuing its ambitious plans to build out the systems to connect all regions. The financial viability of the existing network will continue to improve as traffic grows, but some lines with less traffic and lower prices will continue to face challenges. The use of more flexible demand-based tariffs and regular fare adjustments have a potential role to play. Opportunities to enhance the HSR experience through improved urban connectivity beckon. And the world will continue to learn from China's high-speed rail experience.

www.ingramcontent.com/pod-product-compliance
Lightning Source LLC
Chambersburg PA
CBHW041449210326
41599CB00004B/184